Parveen - 2017
1

Parveen THE SPICE QUEEN

Authentic Indian Cooking

Copyright Parveen Ashraf 2016
Cover Design by Nadim Ashraf
Cover Image by Jack Sharp
Published by FCM PUBLISHING
www.fcmpublishing.co.uk
First printed in the UK – January 2017
ISBN 978-0-9956296-2-2

Contents

MORTAR AND PESTLE

Introduction

*T*he recipes in this cook book are based on the ones that my mother taught me and have been handed down from generation to generation. They are truly authentic and I have tried my absolute best to do my mum proud and keep the recipes to the way she used to cook. The recipes are Kashmiri/Northern Pakistani style with strong aromas, depth of flavour but not necessarily heat. It is a common misconception that good Indian cuisine has to be hot, it doesn't, it just needs to be hot enough. Like I always say when I am teaching cooking, it's meant to be a party in your mouth — not a rave.

My step-by-step recipes are so simple to follow that you will be able to re-create them in your own home with ease. You can choose from the slightly easier option of using one of my spice bags, or if you're feeling a little adventurous you can blend your own spices. These simple recipes will be something you will want to cook again and again and I promise you, that you will never go back to ready-made curry sauces once you have cooked the real thing.

A little bit about me. I was born in Bradford, West Yorkshire, the curry capital of the North in my humble opinion. I am the middle child of seven and certainly lived up to the title of "middle child". I was so full of character and always wanted to be the centre of attention... well, no change there then! Growing up, the focal point of family life was mealtimes, in the evenings mum would make fabulous tasting food and we would all sit around the dinner table, eat and chat, we were like the Asian Waltons!

For some people, the 70's may have been a dark and depressing time in the North, but we had mum's onion bhajis to come home to, which we ate by candlelight. For me, it was a magical time and when my love affair with food began. My passion for good food was further fuelled by my husband whom I married in 1987 and I just loved cooking for him. He would make suggestions and I would tweak my recipes to suit his palate and he always complimented me after every meal. Who doesn't love a compliment... I know I do!

I have three grown up children, who are now aged 26, 25 and 19. I raised my children the way I was raised, with family meals being the focal point of family life. In this fast paced life of fast cars, fast wi-fi and eating on the go, I find that mealtimes are probably the only times we sit together to take a breather, talk about our day and connect with each other. Family meals are so important to me that I actually banned phones at my dinner table, and yes, that includes my husband, well it's the only time I get to pull rank.

I have been catering for most of my adult life but only decided to set up my business in 2008, after having a tumour and completely changing my career path, I decided to follow my passion and cook for a living. So, for nearly a decade now, I have been teaching, demonstrating and catering my glamorous Bollywood Dinner Parties alongside selling my own range of spice mixes. I have been lucky enough to teach Indian cookery in several schools and colleges in the UK as well as Europe.

So now, with this book, I can help you on your gastronomic journey into the art of Indian cuisine. It's easy really, with the right method and the right spice, you can make amazingly tasting authentic food which your friends and family will absolutely love. I really hope you enjoy making the dishes as much as I enjoyed writing the recipes for you.

Culinary Yours

Parveen x

"I feel this picture really encapsulates my mum... it's her signature dessert styled on one of her signature shawls."

Acknowledgements

I am so grateful to so many people who have helped me along my journey in writing this — my first cook book. To my very good friend, Jeannie, whose patience knew no bounds, who read every word, cooked every recipe and was always ever ready on the end of a phone when I needed advice, which was a lot! Also thanks to my brother-in-law, Nadim and my good friend Jack Sharp for their candour, creativity and honesty.

To my three amazing children, who are all so very different in character and personality, and who each individually supported me in their own way; from my eldest son, Imran, who inspired me to write my very first recipe. Having gone to University and needing a taste of home, he was the catalyst that made me put pen to paper, well actually more like finger tips on a keyboard, but you get the idea. Then, Sherine for her proof reading skills and tenacity, when arguing over every single word and comma. Then last but certainly not least, my youngest, Cyrus, who at age 19, is 6ft 2", has hollow legs but whose feedback on the taste was essential to the process.

I also want to thank my wonderful husband, for his endless patience and having faith in me, even when I didn't. Also, I want to thank the woman who took my dreams and turned them into a reality — Taryn, my publisher, who saw potential in me, my book and of course, my recipes.

Naturally, these acknowledgements would not be complete without me thanking my mother. Not only for passing on her passion for cooking but how to do it from the heart with one key, immeasurable, essential ingredient — love.

Fabulous Photographs by Dana from Aldanah Photography

I want to say a very special thank you to the lovely Dana who was a pleasure to work with. We decided from the very first day of the photo shoot to keep the whole creative process authentic. We decided that all the food should be cooked fresh, from scratch and photographed straight away. So that's exactly what we did — I cooked everything in my kitchen, used my own crockery (well mostly, although I did borrow some from friends) and then we just let our creativity take over. Dana and I had a blast, we were in our creative groove; styling the food, getting excited over every shot and best of all, eating the food. I am so thrilled with the way she has made my food come to life.

MY PEARLS OF WISDOM

Before you begin, I would love to share my preparation pearls of wisdom with you.

MAKE TIME:

Always bear in mind that this process is not from a jar or a packet and therefore may take you longer than perhaps you are used to. Some of the dishes, especially the mains, can take up to 1 to 2 hours. I suggest that you open a bottle of wine, put on the radio and enjoy the process (If like me you don't drink wine, stick the kettle on and have a cup of tea — you can take the girl out of Yorkshire but you can't take Yorkshire out of the girl!). Any food that is cooked in a happy relaxed atmosphere will always taste just that little bit more special, so why not cook as a family or with your partner?

REMEMBER THAT THIS IS NOT "FAST FOOD".

Stirring and stir frying is a very important part of the cooking process as the depth of flavour comes from the way the spices are cooked. In Punjabi we actually have one word to describe this cooking technique, it's called "bhun" which actually means to stir the spices continuously on high heat whilst the sauce reduces.

However, not all the recipes are long, some of the starters cook in no time at all. For example, the tandoori chicken and lamb sheesh kebabs — "marination to mouth in 10 minutes".

PREP WELL:

Before you begin, have a read of the recipe and make sure you have the correct ingredients, good quality pans and familiarise yourself with the method. This way you won't be caught off guard or feel flustered!

VENTILATION:

Make sure your kitchen is well ventilated or use an extractor fan. Like a lot of wonderfully flavoured food, the cooking is an aromatic process and the smell of the spices can be easily absorbed. After cooking, I usually light a scented candle to take away any leftover cooking smells. Plus I usually don't go out in the clothes that I cook in... I may be the Spice Queen, but I would much rather smell of Chanel than spice!

Oil, Ghee and Butter

"To ghee or not to ghee" that is the question? I am often asked by my students if I use ghee (purified butter) in my cooking. Traditionally ghee was used in the preparation of many dishes, but these days for a healthier option you can use other oils without compromising the flavour, including Sunflower, Vegetable, Rapeseed, Olive and Coconut oil.

Sometimes to add flavour I use butter, for example in the stock when making rice or to spread on hot chapattis. Some people are taken aback by the amount of oil used, especially in curries. But you need oil to make a good curry as the spices need to be fried to cook them through. If you want a healthier option either halve the amount of oil or drain the oil once the food is cooked. If you cook a curry without oil it tends to taste like a spicy casserole and will not have that depth of flavour that a good curry has.

SOME TOP TIPS TO HELP WITH YOUR COOKING

When I was teaching cooking, I usually gave my students and clients certain rules of thumb. These were taught to me by my mother. There is no rhyme nor reason as to why they work and why I cook this way, except to say that they do!

◆ Wherever possible, always try and use a stainless steel pan. Not a non-stick one. Stainless steel pans really help when we are reducing the sauce when cooking curries and rice.

◆ Always use a wooden spoon when cooking main dishes like curry and rice. There is a lot of stirring to do, so buy one that you are comfortable with and then hold on to it. Plus if you use a metal spoon, it can create a slightly metallic taste when used with a stainless steel pan.

◆ If you like your food hot, don't be tempted to add extra red chilli powder, just add a few roughly chopped green chillies and simmer through. They are gentler on your stomach than red chilli powder.

◆ Use fresh ginger and garlic, it's worth all that peeling and chopping. See my chapter on "The Importance of Ginger and Garlic" on page 21.

◆ For many of my main dishes, I use tinned tomatoes. The reason being is that the tomato juice creates a lovely rich sauce as a base. This is my personal preference and in my experience works well.

◆ Coriander versus Fenugreek Leaves. Generally speaking use dry fenugreek leaves to add flavour to vegetable dishes like Aloo Gobi, Okra and Vegetable Curry. Meat dishes such as Lamb Bhuna, Chicken Masala and Lamb Chops taste better with fresh coriander.

Garam Masala

This is probably the most used of all the spices in my meat & curry recipes. Garam Masala, literally translated, means "warm spice" because although very strong in flavour it has very little heat. There are many recipes for garam masala; they differ from region to region and in my experience, from family to family. Of course, if you don't have time, you can buy ready-made but I don't think it is a patch on home ground and you really can taste the difference.

To make my version of garam masala, I use a packet of the whole spice mix, this contains all of the 7 spices you will need; you just need to adjust the quantities. Take out half of the cinnamon sticks, bay leaves and black cardamom as these can make it taste slightly bitter. Dry fry them on a low heat in a non-stick pan for 30 seconds to a minute, then add a little at a time into your coffee grinder and grind to a powder. Store in an airtight jar, this will ensure that it remains fresh for up to a year.

Cloves

Whole black pepper

Cumin

Coriander seeds

Black cardamom

Cinnamon

Bay leaves

Ingredients for Indian Cuisine

*F*resh, quality ingredients are essential when making a really good authentic Indian dish. In all my years of teaching cooking, one thing that would fluster my students is the ingredient list used when making Indian food. But these days nearly everything is readily available in many of the major supermarkets; they now have "World Food" aisles selling most of the ingredients you would need to cook using this cookbook. Many of the ingredients needed are commonplace such as garlic, chilli, cumin etc. Even fresh coriander is usually on sale in the fresh food section. However, when it comes to dry spices many people are not sure what to buy.

Spices

If you can manage it, try and shop in an Asian grocers, as they will have ALL the spices you need to cook my recipes. They sell a wide range of whole spices as well as powdered spices. Some spices are quite good when shop bought but for others, its best to buy the whole spices, roast and grind them yourself and then store in an airtight jar. To grind your own spices; the best method is to use a coffee grinder, but a word of warning, once used to grind spices you won't be able to grind coffee again (unless you want spicy coffee!!). For that reason I have a coffee grinder, which is dedicated to grinding my spices in my kitchen. I am also lucky enough to own an industrial grinder for my spice bags, well, that's the perk of having your own range of spices.

CUMIN

I use cumin quite a lot — I love it. I use it to flavour yoghurt, potatoes, rice and even roast vegetables. Ready ground cumin is easily available in large supermarkets and it's quite acceptable, but try buying whole cumin seeds, to roast and grind yourself — it's a different level of flavour.

TANDOORI POWDER

Tandoori powder is reddish in colour but has no real flavour. It tastes like a very mild version of paprika and is usually used to add colour to dishes like tandoori chicken. I sometimes add to my meat dishes to enhance the colour.

CORIANDER SEEDS

This spice has a slightly gingery and lemony flavour. I use it in addition to garam masala to flavour a lot of my meat dish recipes. As with cumin, you can buy ready ground coriander powder, but for a more authentic flavour buy whole coriander seeds and roast and grind them at home.

POMEGRANATE SEED POWDER

This as the name suggests is made from drying out pomegranate seeds and grinding them into a powder. It has a sour lemon-like flavour and if you cannot get hold of any you can use a little lemon juice in its place. Pomegranate seed powder is usually used in starter dishes like samosas, spicy potato cakes and onion bhajis.

FRESH CORIANDER

This ethnic herb is a must in many Indian dishes and many of my recipes too. When shopping for coriander take a piece and squish it between your thumb and index finger, this releases the lovely smell. If it smells good, it will taste good. Also, remember most of the flavour is in the stalk which you can use whilst cooking. As for the leaves, add them at the end of the cooking process or use as a garnish.

CARDAMOM

I use a lot of cardamom in my desserts but not so much in my starters or mains. However, I know many other people that use it in meat and rice dishes. I think the strong flavour takes away from the taste of the "spicy" spice, if you get my meaning? But you will notice nearly all the dessert recipes in this cook book contain cardamom, I love the taste with sweet dishes.

The role of salt in Indian Cooking

Salt is a vital ingredient in my recipes, without it you'll just get the heat of chillies without the flavour. Many people are surprised at the amount of salt required in my dishes, but if you pro-rata it down, you are probably eating less salt in a portion of chicken curry than you are in a bag of crisps. If you suffer from high blood pressure, try cutting the amount down by half or cut down your portion size... just have a little of something you fancy. However, these days I don't tend to use table salt as it makes me thirsty. I usually use sea salt. I am unsure about the science behind it as I am not a scientist, but my son is, he graduated with a chemical engineering degree a few years ago and explained the difference between what we call table salt, which is Sodium Chloride (not good for your body) as opposed to natural sea salt (which is organic and better for you).

Himalayan Sea Salt and Mum

Recently, I find that there is a trend for using Pink Himalayan Sea Salt, which you can buy in many high-end supermarkets. As the name suggests it was originally sourced from the foot of the Himalayan Mountains, which stretch from India, China, Nepal to Pakistan. Many people believe Himalayan Sea Salt is the purest salt that can be found on the planet ... and one of those believers was my mother. In fact the last time mum stayed with me she mentioned for the umpteenth time how dad used to bring her large rocks of natural Himalayan Sea Salt which she'd spend hours grinding the good old fashioned way, in a mortar and pestle. Well, my mum may have used old fashioned method but she was using Himalayan Sea Salt half a century before the rest of us, so it would seem my mum was way ahead of her time.

Some commonly used herbs and spices

CHILLI POWDER

Chilli powder is made from drying out and grinding fresh red chilli peppers. There are various levels of heat to chillies; the smaller the chilli the more powerful the flavour, the larger the chilli the milder the flavour. When cooking use a medium heat chilli powder and use more. Extra hot chilli powder can damage your stomach if not properly cooked.

TURMERIC

Turmeric is used in most of my curry recipes, especially meat dishes and is very good for you, as it can act as an antiseptic. Even as an adult when I was poorly my mum gave me turmeric milk to heal me from the inside, mum told me that back in the day when she was young her mother would make a turmeric paste to apply on any wounds. Bright yellow in colour, be careful, it can stain clothes.

DRY FENUGREEK LEAVES

These dried green leaves have a very strong, pungent aroma. You could buy fresh and dry it out but ready-made in packets are usually good quality. When adding to dishes give it a squeeze in your fingertips first to release the flavours. I must admit I am a fan of it and use it in a lot of my vegetarian dishes as it adds real depth.

Some commonly used Asian Vegetables and Pulses

OKRA (LADIES FINGERS)

Okra is an acquired taste but nevertheless a flavoursome vegetable that is commonly used in Indian cooking. Okra is firm to the touch and has a slightly furry feel. It can turn "slimy" if water is added whilst cooking. You will need to wash it while whole, dry with a cloth and then slice.

COURGETTES

This vegetable is becoming more popular of late and is widely available now. Courgettes have a delicate flavour and soak up spices really well. They are used in my recipe for mixed vegetable curry. When buying courgettes make sure they are firm to the touch. You can either peel them or cook with the skin on.

AUBERGINE

This beautiful purple vegetable is used in my mixed vegetable recipe. Aubergines do not have to be peeled, just slice and use in the recipe. They can come in various sizes. If you cannot find fresh, you can use frozen, but I find that fresh is best.

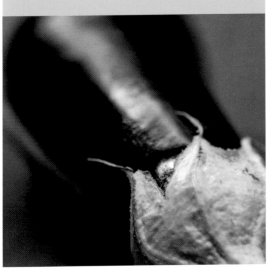

RED SPLIT LENTILS

This is probably the most commonly used lentil and is used to make "Tarka Daal". It is orange in colour when dry but turns a beautiful golden yellow when cooked.

CHANNA DAAL

This is a yellow lentil which has a nutty flavour and takes quite a long time to cook, but if you soak it first it reduces down the cooking time. Most large supermarkets stock this type of lentil.

CHICK PEAS

I nearly always use tinned chick peas as they taste just as good and keep their shape when cooked. The canned chick peas can vary in size, but try and buy the larger ones as they seem to work better in my recipes.

"To cook chick peas — see recipe for channa masala on page 85, a simple and easy dish. Serve it with cumin buttered rice, cucumber raita and enjoy!"

The Importance of Ginger and Garlic

Many of my recipes for curries require the use of ginger and/or garlic and more often than not they are used together. Most commonly used in meat and main dishes but not so much in the starters. The history probably lies in the fact that people would use ginger and garlic to preserve the meat as well as warding off bacteria that thrive in hot climates.

Always use fresh wherever and whenever possible

When cooking the recipes in this book try wherever and whenever possible to use fresh garlic bulbs and fresh root ginger as opposed to frozen, ready-made pastes and powders. When buying garlic bulbs make sure the whole bulb is intact and is quite firm to the touch, white with streaks of purple or just white garlic is fine. Again with fresh root ginger, make sure it is firm to the touch. Fresh root ginger looks like a mini bark of a tree and is light brown in colour.

Alternatives to Fresh

Recently I have been experimenting with ready-made frozen ginger and garlic. They are a good alternative to fresh and actually work quite well with Indian cuisine and my recipes. If you don't have the time to buy and prepare fresh ginger and garlic many of the larger supermarkets sell it in frozen form, so give them a go. You can buy ones that contain 100% ginger and 100% garlic, read the ingredients before you buy. Other alternatives to fresh garlic and ginger are pastes but they usually contain preservatives including citric acid and this tends to leave an acidic aftertaste. As a last resort you could use ginger and garlic powders which you will find in the spice section in most supermarkets. Powders have a long shelf life but in terms of their flavour they are a poor relation to the real thing.

Methods to Prepare Garlic

There are several ways to prepare garlic. One of the easiest is probably using a garlic crusher. I have got this super duper garlic crusher that doesn't even require you to peel the garlic, just pop in a clove and give it a good squeeze ... simple! In complete contrast to this is the traditional way that my mum used to crush garlic and I still do today, which is to use a mortar and pestle. Peel the garlic; a quick tip on how to peel garlic, flatten the garlic using the flat side of your knife, and squish it a little, then use your thumb to peel away the thin papery-like skin, peel from the ridged end of the garlic. Once the garlic cloves are peeled place into the pestle, add a little salt to stop it slipping about, which tends to happen as you bash away. I find the salt helps to create a great paste, just remember to deduct the amount of salt you have used from the recipe. Don't make the mistake I did when I first learnt to cook, I added a teaspoon of salt to crush the garlic, then added another 2 teaspoons in the chicken masala. Not good, but lesson learnt. Another common method to prepare garlic is to use a mini chopper or blender, peel the garlic, add 3 tablespoons of water to help the blending process and blitz for 2 to 3 minutes or until smooth.

Methods to Prepare Root Ginger

Again, as with garlic, there are several ways to prepare fresh root ginger. To peel the ginger you can either scrape away the tough brown skin using a knife or use the edge of a spoon which will suffice. You can grate the ginger using the small side of a cheese grater and this works quite well with the "stringy" flesh of root ginger. Or you can use the traditional method of a mortar and pestle. Peel the ginger, cut it into ½ cm slices, widthways and crush. No need to add salt as it easily breaks down. And of course you can use an electric mini chopper or blender, just add 3 tablespoons of water and blitz for a couple of minutes.

Making Home-made Frozen Ginger and Garlic

Sometimes when I have the time and inclination, I peel my ginger and garlic en masse and freeze it in ice cube trays. It may be time consuming and frankly quite a "smelly" task but once I have my own stash in the freezer, I feel a real sense of achievement. Needless to say once you have used the ice cube trays to freeze your ginger and garlic they are no good for anything else. The smell is just ingested by the plastic. To make your own stash; peel the garlic and ginger, cut into 1cm pieces, blitz in a blender with some water for at least 2 to 3 minutes or until you have a smooth paste. Carefully pour into ice cube trays and freeze. Once frozen, take out the frozen pieces and put into plastic freezer bags. It's best to double bag as the smell is quite potent and you don't want your freezer to be taken over by the smell.

Starters

Whilst these are called starters you can make them for snacks at any time of the day. The good news is that some of the starters can be cooked quite quickly, for example, the tandoori chicken and lamb sheesh kebabs — marination to mouth in 10 minutes!

Many of the meat dishes can be cooked and frozen without any compromise to the taste. Just heat up in a microwave or oven and enjoy. If you are busy, which most of us are these days, just do some batch cooking on a Sunday when you have time, cook as per the recipe and pop in the freezer. As with most frozen food use within three months. I have been known to forget about food in my freezer and as my son Cyrus would say "remember mum, it's a freezer — not a time machine!"

You can either buy your own spices or buy a spice bag containing all the spices highlighted in red from my website:

www.the-spicequeen.com

Lamb Samosa in Crispy Pastry

Spicy minced lamb, potato and peas wrapped in triangle shaped pastry and deep fried till crispy. This is a simple take on the traditional samosas which are quite difficult to make and quite a long process. But I really wanted to include the recipe in the book. So I adapted the recipe using ready-made spring roll pastry, making it easier to follow. Once you have mastered the technique you will want to show off your skills and make them time and time again. Sometimes in real emergencies, when I just don't have the time to cook from scratch, I have been known to buy ready-made samosas from the Asian supermarkets. They taste quite good but personally I find them a little too salty and spicy, that's why it is always better to make your own, that way you are in charge of the density of spices.

PREPARATION TIME: 50 MINUTES COOKING TIME: 5 MINUTES (TO FRY) MAKES ABOUT 45 SAMOSAS

Ingredients

500 g of good quality lamb mince

2 large white potatoes – diced into 1 cm squares

3 medium sized onions – diced small

200 g frozen or fresh garden peas

2 fresh tomatoes – diced

1 tsp salt

1 tsp chilli powder

3 tsp coriander powder

1 tsp cumin powder

1 tsp pomegranate seed powder

2 tbsp oil

2 beaten eggs – to use as a glue to bind the pastry

30 sheets of spring roll pastry

1 litre of oil to fry

Method

1. In a large stainless steel pan add the mince, oil, spices, tomatoes, onions and salt, bring to the boil and simmer for 10 mins.

2. Turn heat on high and cook for 10 minutes until the onions and tomatoes have broken down and the meat has cooked. Add the potatoes and keep stirring on high for 5 mins, or until potatoes have nearly cooked.

3. Add the peas and stir the mixture together, cook for a further 5 minutes on medium heat. Taste for seasoning, then simmer with lid on for a further 2 to 3 minutes.

4. Transfer the samosa filling into a large bowl, allowing it to cool down.

5. Cut the pastry into 3 equal strips, gently peel two strips together (diagram 1). Fold the pastry over (diagram 2), brush with egg (diagram 3) then fold over again to create a triangular pocket (diagram 4). Add two level tbsp of the mince filling (diagram 5) and fold over the flap to seal the samosa (diagram 6).

6. Heat the oil in a wok or a deep heavy-bottomed saucepan. Deep fry the samosas for 3 to 4 minutes, till golden brown then drain on kitchen paper before serving.

Parveen's Top Tip

You can make samosas to step 5 and pop them into the freezer for up to three months. Then to fry, take them out of the freezer, allow them to thaw completely and fry as per step 6.

Tandoori Chicken Drumsticks

This recipe may be described as "Tandoori" which actually means a clay oven, but seeing as many of us don't have one of those, a bog standard conventional oven will have to do. Tandoori Chicken Drumsticks are great to serve at a party and best of all they are so easy to prepare with very little actual cooking. Just marinate the chicken and pop in the oven. I am often asked so many questions about how long tandoori chicken needs to marinate for. Is it overnight, is it two hours or is it ten minutes? Actually, it's all three. The longer you marinate the chicken for the more tender it tends to be.

PREPARATION TIME: 10 MINUTES   COOKING TIME: 40 MINUTES   SERVES APPROX — 5-6 PEOPLE

Ingredients

10 chicken drumsticks

1 tbsp plain yoghurt

1 tsp of chilli powder

1 tsp of tandoori powder

1 tsp coriander seed powder

½ tsp chilli flakes

1 tsp salt

2 tsp lemon juice, fresh or bottled

1 tbsp vegetable or sunflower oil

Method

1. With a sharp knife, carefully score the fleshiest part of the drumstick, this allows all the lovely spices to be absorbed into the chicken.

2. In a large bowl add the yoghurt, salt, lemon juice, all the spices, oil and mix together — this is the marinade. Now add chicken pieces and coat thoroughly.

3. Leave to marinate at room temperature for 30 mins (allowing flavours to fuse together).

4. Place chicken in a baking tray and cover with aluminium foil, cook in hot oven at 200°C for 30 minutes.

5. Now take the foil off and you will notice all the juices from the chicken and the yoghurt have created a spicy stock, do not drain this as you will need this liquid to baste the chicken pieces.

6. Continue to cook the chicken for a further 10 to 15 minutes, keep turning and basting the chicken in its own juices till tender. The liquid should reduce and the chicken should be slightly crispy.

Parveen's Top Tip

If you like it spicy, just add an extra tsp of chilli powder or chilli flakes, which also makes the chicken look even more appetising. And if you are not a fan of chicken drumsticks, you can use chicken thighs, they are just as lovely and tender. Try adding potatoes to the recipe, just add 10 to 12 new potatoes cut into halves at stage 2. It's amazing because as the dish cooks, they have all the flavour of the chicken but they are potatoes. When you baste the chicken, your potatoes will also crisp up and hey presto, you have amazing tasting tandoori roast potatoes! Another flavour dimension is to roughly slice some red onions and add with the potatoes, again, amazingly crispy and sweet as they caramelise with the chicken stock.

Pan Fried Tandoori Chicken

These spicy, tender tasting medallions of chicken are healthy, quick and easy to make. They make great starters that can be eaten as part of a healthy diet if you are watching the calories. They are best served in warm pitta bread with plain salty yoghurt and salad. I often make this as a main meal for my two boys, who are a little bit obsessed with the gym these days. It's a perfectly packed protein meal. This recipe also works really well as BBQ tandoori chicken. To barbeque, cut the chicken fillets into approximately 2 cm cubes and cook on skewers as you would normally do.

PREPARATION TIME: 10 MINUTES	COOKING TIME: 10 MINUTES	MAKES BETWEEN 20 TO 25 PIECES

Ingredients

2 chicken breasts

1 tbsp plain yoghurt

1 tsp of chilli powder

1 tsp of tandoori powder

½ tsp of coriander seed powder

½ tsp of chilli flakes

1 tsp salt

2 tsp lemon juice, fresh or bottled

1 tbsp vegetable or sunflower oil

Method

1. Cut chicken into medallions (1 cm thick) the pieces should be roughly the same size but if they are not, don't worry you can just cook the smaller pieces for less time.

2. In a large bowl, add the yoghurt, salt, lemon juice, chilli flakes, chilli powder, coriander seed powder, tandoori powder and mix together — this is the marinade. Now add chicken pieces and coat thoroughly. Leave to marinade at room temperature for 30 minutes (allowing flavours to fuse together).

3. Add 1 or 2 tbsp of oil into a frying pan and heat till oil is hot.

4. Carefully place chicken pieces in the pan. Make sure you leave space between each piece, so you should be able to pan fry 6 or 7 depending on the size of your pan.

5. Cook on high heat for about 1 min on each side to seal the chicken, then a further 2 minutes on each side to make sure the chicken is cooked through.

6. Clean the frying pan with kitchen paper between each batch of chicken and continue to cook all the chicken. Either serve straight away or store in a tupperware with a lid to keep in all the moisture.

Parveen's Top Tip

If you have a busy life, you can marinate the chicken and it will keep in the fridge for 2 days. Then just pan fry and eat. Or you can make a big batch and freeze the chicken and all you have to do is take it out of the freezer, pop into the microwave on high for 2 mins and you are good to go!

Chappal Kebab

These meaty kebabs are a very popular starter at weddings, parties and family gatherings ...well basically any special occasion. They are named "Chappal" after the word for a flat sandal in Punjabi — phonetically pronounced as chapl. My mum used to deep fry them, however, to be kind to my heart I pan fry them with a small amount of oil. Sometimes I grill them when I am trying to cut down the fat content. I like to serve them topped with sautéed onions, cumin roast potatoes and cucumber raita.

PREPARATION TIME: 10 MINUTES	COOKING TIME: 4 TO 5 MINUTES	MAKES BETWEEN 15 TO 18 PIECES

Ingredients

800 g lamb or mutton mince

200 g chicken mince

1 finely grated onion

2 green chillies, finely chopped

1 to 1 ½ tsp salt (or to taste)

3 tsp coriander powder

1 tsp cumin powder

2 tsp pomegranate seed powder — optional

2 tsp fenugreek leaves

2 tbsp chopped fresh coriander

2 tbsp of vegetable oil to pan fry

Method

1. Add all of the ingredients (apart from the oil) in a large bowl and mix thoroughly. Best to use your hands, if you are not a fan of touching raw meat — just wear some gloves. Allow the mixture to rest at room temperature for 10 mins.

2. Take about 2 tbsp (50 g) of the mixture, shape into patties using your palms and fingers. To achieve perfectly flat and even kebabs, make a small ball with the meat, place in between some cling film and press down using a dinner plate.

3. To pan fry add a few drops of oil into a non-stick pan. Turn the heat on high and carefully add one kebab at a time. You should be able to cook 3 or 4 at one time.

4. On high heat cook for about 2 mins, this will seal and cook the meat, turn over and cook for 2 mins on the other side. You will notice that meat juices will ooze from the kebabs, do not be tempted to drain off as this will reduce down as the kebabs cooks.

5. Turn the heat down to medium and cook for a further 2 to 3 mins on each side, this allows the kebabs to cook through.

6. Serve hot with cool cucumber raita and lemon & coriander salad.

BBQ Tip

These lamb sheesh kebabs taste amazing cooked on the barbeque on a hot summers day. To barbeque, follow step 1 of the recipe; take 2 tablespoons (50 g) of the mixture and carefully wrap the meat around a barbeque skewer. Moisten your hands with a little oil first to stop the meat sticking to your hands. Or shape into burgers and cook on barbeque as desired. I recommend that you seal the meat in a pan for about 30 seconds on each side first, this will stop the meat sticking to your barbeque grill. These kebabs are my son Cyrus's favourite starter, he loves them in a brioche bun with sautéed onions, covered in cheese and with a little chilli sauce... absolutely delicious!

Onion Bhajis

There are so many different recipes for onion bhajis but I think this is the simplest and easiest, they turn out light and crispy every time. I have used this recipe hundreds of times and I always add potatoes to mine. In fact, I don't think I have ever made an onion bhaji with just onions. Bhajis are so popular and a real crowd pleaser. Serve them with a minty yoghurt or green chilli dip. Another option is to try the East meets West method — in two slices of buttered bread with believe it or not, tomato ketchup. All my three children love their Bhaji Butties. Onion bhajis are gluten free as the base ingredient is gram flour, which is made from chick peas. They are the perfect little starter for vegetarians, vegans and pescatarians, however be forewarned, they are highly addictive!

PREPARATION TIME: 10 MINUTES + 30 MINUTES FOR MIXTURE TO REST   COOKING TIME: 10 MINUTES   MAKES 28 TO 30 MEDIUM SIZED BHAJIS

Ingredients

250 g gram flour

2 medium sized onions — halved & thinly sliced

2 medium sized potatoes — thinly sliced

2 tsp coriander seed powder

1 tsp chilli powder

2 tsp dried fenugreek leaves (optional)

1 tsp pomegranate seed powder

½ tsp cumin powder

1 tsp salt

3 tbsp of fresh coriander — chopped

Few drops of lemon juice

1 litre of oil (for frying)

Method

1. Sieve the flour into a large mixing bowl, add the salt, chilli powder, coriander seed powder, pomegranate seed powder, cumin and lemon juice.

2. Add 125 ml water to the gram flour, mix with a wooden spoon to make a batter. The consistency should be smooth and similar to double cream.

3. Add the chopped coriander, fenugreek leaves, potatoes and onion, mix well, making sure that all the potatoes and onions are covered in the batter. Cover and leave to stand for 30 mins.

4. Heat oil in a wok or deep frying pan, drop a teaspoon of batter into the hot oil and fry. You can fry 6 or 7 at a time, depending on how large your pan is.

5. Deep fry for 3 to 5 minutes or until golden brown — turning once or twice to ensure they brown and crisp up on all sides. Take out using a slotted spoon and metal sieve, give them a good shake and drain onto kitchen roll.

Parveen's Top Tip

To make light and crispy bhajis, the batter has to be quite thin. I have a little tongue twister I like to use: "The thinner the batter, the better the bhaji". Use it is as a mantra because it really works. You can use other vegetables for bhajis, sometimes called Pakora. Try red peppers, cauliflower or just potatoes. Just thinly slice the vegetables, cover in the batter and deep fry.

TOP TIP FOR FRYING To make sure the oil is at the right temperature, drop in a piece of potato, if it floats to the top within 5 seconds it's the right temperature, if it stays at the bottom then the oil is too cold. And when frying, fry on high for 1 min, turn the temperature down and fry on medium for 3 mins and finish off on high for the last minute. This ensures that the bhajis are crispy on the outside and cooked in the middle.

Fish Pakoras

These are small pieces of white fish covered in gram flour and deep fried till crispy. This recipe for fish pakoras is easy, quick and tastes divine. I usually serve these as appetizers when I am having a dinner party. Use whatever fish you like, any white fish will do. And if you have friends that are coeliacs and have a gluten free diet, feed them these Pakoras and they will love you forever. The batter with it's beautiful yellow colour is made from gram flour, which is actually chick pea flour, hence it has no wheat — Oh Joy!

PREPARATION TIME: 10 + 10 MINUTES   COOKING TIME: 3 TO 5 MINUTES TO FRY   MAKES APPROX 10 — 12

Ingredients

100 g of gram flour

100 g cod or any white fillet of fish

½ tsp salt

1 tsp chilli powder

1 tsp of coriander powder

1 tsp fenugreek leaves (optional)

1 tsp of lemon juice, fresh or bottled

1 tbsp of fresh chopped coriander leaves

500 ml of sunflower oil or vegetable oil — to fry

Method

1. Sieve the flour into a mixing bowl; add the salt, chilli powder, coriander powder, fenugreek leaves and lemon juice.

2. Add 100 ml water to the gram flour, mixing slowly as you add the water, the consistency should be smooth and similar to double cream. Add the chopped coriander, mix well, cover and leave to stand for 10 mins.

3. Cut fish into desired sized pieces preferably 1 ½ inch squares.

4. Heat oil in a frying pan or wok. Dip the fish in batter and deep fry. You can fry 6 or 7 at a time, depending on how large your pan is. Deep fry for 3 to 4 minutes or until lightly golden brown.

5. Take out using a metal sieve to shake off the excess oil, drain on kitchen roll.

6. Best eaten hot, served with a mint chutney and a salad.

Parveen's Top Tip

If you want to push the boat out, you can try this recipe with small pieces of salmon. For extra flavour squeeze a little fresh lemon juice on the pakoras just before you serve them, it adds a real zing. To test the oil to see if it is the correct temperature to fry; dip a piece of bread into the batter and drop into the oil. If it floats to the to the top within 3 to 4 seconds then the oil is the correct temperature to fry. If the bread sinks to the bottom the oil is too cold. If the batter splits then the oil is too hot. For best results use a wok.

Chick Pea Spicy Salad (Chaat)

Commonly just referred to as "chaat" — this is a fat-free tangy tasting starter which I usually serve with samosas. Considering it contains no added fats, it tastes surprisingly good. When I was trying to lose weight after having my daughter it was my "go to" food and guess what, she loves it too! Chick pea chaat is a popular street food which I first had as a teenager in the bazaars of Rawalpindi. It requires hardly any cooking and can be served cold or at room temperature. Also, it can be made a day or two in advance and will happily sit in the refrigerator until it's time to serve. It's best eaten with cumin yoghurt drizzled with tamarind sauce.

PREPARATION TIME: 10 MINUTES   COOKING TIME: 10 MINUTES   SERVES APPROX 4–6 AS A STARTER WITH SAMOSAS

Ingredients

2 tins of chick peas (400 g) washed & drained

2 or 3 medium sized white potatoes

½ tsp chilli flakes

½ tsp chilli powder

2 tsp of cumin powder

2 tsp of pomegranate seed powder

1 tsp salt

3 tbsp of chopped coriander leaves

3 tsp of freshly squeezed lemon juice

Method

1. Peel and dice the potatoes into 2 cm cubes.

2. Boil the potatoes in slightly salted water for 8 to 10 mins or until they are cooked. Do not over boil, as they need to be intact and hold their shape. Remember they will continue to cook in the residual heat.

3. Empty the drained chick peas into a large bowl. Add the salt, chilli flakes, chilli powder, pomegranate seed powder, cumin, lemon juice and fresh coriander leaves. Mix the ingredients together until the chick peas are thoroughly and evenly coated in the spice mixture.

4. Now add the cooked potatoes and gently mix together.

5. Serve individually in bowls, pour the cumin yoghurt on top and drizzle with some tamarind sauce — as the smaller photos suggest.

Parveen's Top Tip

The tamarind sauce gives the sharp, tangy flavour that is associated with chaat. Frankly, it really shouldn't be eaten without it. To make the sauce see page 117. Tamarind sauce and paste is now easily available in ethnic food stores and some large supermarkets. However, in a dire emergency I have used brown sauce as a substitute — well, needs must!

Bombay Potato Cakes (Aloo Tikkah)

These tangy, soft potato cakes are a firm favourite of my sister's, she makes them quite often when we visit. They satisfy the need for something light and spicy. They can be easily prepared and made in advance and all you have to do is pop them in the microwave for a couple of minutes and they are ready to serve. These are fabulous little starters with a cucumber raita or a cumin yoghurt.

PREPARATION TIME: 10 MINUTES	COOKING TIME: 20 MINUTES	MAKES APPROX 15—18 CAKES

Ingredients

4 medium sized white potatoes (peeled and diced into 1 cm cubes)

2 medium sized onions, very finely diced (red or white)

1 tsp of salt

1 tbsp of roughly ground cumin

1 tsp of chilli flakes

A handful of chopped fresh coriander

2 tsp of pomegranate seed powder

3 to 4 tbsp of sunflower or vegetable oil (to fry)

2 eggs — beaten

Method

1. Boil the potatoes in salted water for 10 mins or till slightly al dente.

2. Drain potatoes and mash roughly with a fork or potato masher, you don't need a smooth mash, in fact it's quite nice to have different sized bits of potato.

3. Add the salt, chilli flakes, pomegranate seed powder, cumin, fresh coriander and onions. Mix all the ingredients together until thoroughly mixed with the potato, season to taste and set aside.

4. In a bowl thoroughly beat the eggs until they have a fluffy consistency.

5. With damp hands, take approximately 2 tbsp of the potato mixture and shape into patties using fingers and palms of your hand.

6. Cover with the egg on both sides and pan fry for 1 minute on one side then gently turn them over and fry for another minute until lightly golden brown. You can fry a few at one time.

Parveen's Top Tip

Just remember when you are mashing the potatoes roughly mash them, this gives them a great texture. If you want a little variety add a couple of tbsp of frozen or fresh peas.

Cumin Roast Potatoes

This simple, tasty recipe was given to me by my sister-in-law, or rather should I say, I pinched the recipe and am quite happy to take the credit for it, naughty me! She made them one Christmas along with a fabulous tandoori turkey. I couldn't believe how simple the recipe was but sometimes the simplest recipes are the best. I have cooked these potatoes umpteen times for my family, friends and clients. I usually make them as an accompaniment to Tandoori Chicken or with Chappal Kebabs.

PREPARATION TIME: 5 MINUTES   COOKING TIME: 20 MINUTES   SERVES APPROX 6—8

Ingredients

1 kg of new potatoes or baby potatoes

1 tsp of coarsely ground cumin seeds

1 tsp of coarsely ground coriander seeds

½ tsp of salt

2 tbsp of vegetable or sunflower oil

Method

1. Pre-heat oven to 200°C / gas mark 6.

2. Boil the potatoes in salted water for approx. 5 minutes or till they are half cooked. You can cut the potatoes in half if you wish or if they are small, just leave them whole.

3. In a large bowl, mix the coriander, cumin and salt, then using your hands thoroughly mix the potatoes so they are coated in the lovely spices.

4. Add oil to baking tray, place the potatoes in tray.

5. Cook in oven for 20 to 30 minutes or until cooked through. Keep turning the potatoes allowing them to crisp up evenly.

Parveen's Top Tip

If you do not like skins on your potatoes then you can use larger ones, just peel and dice into 2 inch cubes you will not need to boil them, add spice mix and roast in the oven. I often use large baking potatoes, cut into wedges. The recipe calls for 1kg of potatoes which is about 2 lbs. If you don't want to make that much just half the recipe.

HEALTHY VERSION: If you are being really healthy and watching the fat content, just use a quarter tsp of oil, which will just lightly coat the potatoes and then you can enjoy your carbs...guilt free!

Main Dishes

There is a huge variety of meat dishes that I could teach you to cook, but these are the most popular. One unique feature of Kashmiri style main dishes is that meat and vegetables are often cooked together in one curry sauce. However, it is important to know which meats and vegetables do work together....but you don't need to worry about that as I have done all the hard work for you. These recipes have been tried and tested by me, my sister and mum for over 30 years — I can assure you, they work every time.

I am not a vegetarian or pescatarian, I suppose I am what they call a flexatarian, I like the flavour of meat but I am not a fan of the texture. Hence I like to add potatoes to many of my dishes so that I can enjoy the flavour of the meat in potato — now that's what you call a win-win situation. Don't take my word for it, try these dishes for yourself and you will know what I mean.

You can either buy your own spices or buy a spice bag containing all the spices highlighted in red from my website:

www.the-spicequeen.com

Chicken Masala

This is probably one of the most popular curries in the UK to date. In all my years of cooking for dinner parties and clients, chicken masala just has to be on the menu. You may know it as Chicken "tikkah" Masala, which is actually not a traditional Asian dish, it was actually invented in Britain so don't be surprised if you meet an Asian that hasn't tried it before. But we just say masala as masala means sauce, and this dish is just chicken in a sauce — simple.

PREPARATION TIME: 10 MINUTES   COOKING TIME: 40 MINUTES   SERVES APPROX 6—8

Ingredients

3 medium sized chicken fillets (1 kg approx)

2 medium sized onions — thinly sliced

1 tin chopped tomatoes — 400 g

6 cloves of garlic — crushed

6 tbsp of vegetable oil

2 tsp mild chilli powder

2 tsp garam masala

¼ tsp turmeric powder

1 tsp tandoori powder

2 cm cube fresh root ginger — grated

2 tsp salt

3 tbsp of fresh coriander (stalk and leaves)

Method

1. Heat the oil in a heavy based steel pan and add onions. Fry the onions for 5 to 10 minutes or until they are a golden brown.

2. On medium heat add ginger and garlic, stir in and cook through for 1 minute.

3. Now add chilli powder, tandoori powder, garam masala, turmeric and salt, stir fry for 1 minute. Keep the heat on medium and enjoy the lovely aromas as the spices release all their flavours.

4. Add tomatoes and cook on medium heat for 10 minutes, keep stirring, if the sauce sticks add a dash of water. The oil will separate and the sauce should have a thick consistency now.

5. Simmer for 5 minutes allowing all the flavours to infuse.

6. Add chicken pieces, stir well, and make sure that all the chicken is covered in the sauce. Turn heat up to high and continue stirring for 10 minutes. If sauce sticks, add a dash of water. Do not leave at this point; just keep stirring on high heat.

7. Add 100 ml of boiling water, add the coriander, stir through and simmer for 10 minutes.

Parveen's Top Tip

You can use boneless pieces of chicken thighs for this recipes, they tend to be a lot more moist. Or try using half chicken breasts and half chicken thighs, that's a good combination — me thinks.

Traditional Chicken Methi (Chicken with Fenugreek)

When I have been busy and neglected my husband I will often make this for him as a peace offering. Although it is a chicken curry it is usually made with the curry sauce being quite "runny" and the fenugreek adds a real earthy, fuller flavour to the dish. I also use a whole chicken that has been carefully cut into pieces by my butcher. I will use all the pieces including the wings and neck as the flavour from the bones helps to flavour the sauce. I serve it with hot chapattis or naan bread.

PREPARATION TIME: 10 MINUTES	COOKING TIME: 40 MINUTES	SERVES APPROX 6–8

Ingredients

1 whole chicken cut into pieces or 1 kg of drumstick & thigh pieces

2 medium sized onions — thinly sliced

1 tin chopped tomatoes 400 g — blitzed in a blender

6 cloves of garlic — crushed

5 tbsp of vegetable oil

2 cm fresh root ginger — grated

4 tsp dried fenugreek leaves

2 tsp mild chilli powder

2 tsp of garam masala

¼ tsp turmeric powder

2 tsp salt

Method

1. Heat the oil in the pan and add onions. Fry the onions until they are a golden brown. On medium heat, add ginger and garlic. Stir in and cook through for 1 minute.

2. Add chilli powder, garam masala, turmeric and salt, add a splash of water, so that the chillies do not burn, stir fry for another minute.

3. Add the tomatoes and cook on medium heat for 10 minutes, keep stirring. The oil will separate and the sauce should have a thick consistency now.

4. Add all the chicken pieces, stir well. Turn heat up to high and continue stirring for 10 minutes, you will notice liquid oozing from the chicken pieces, this is ok, just keep stirring and it will dry out in the cooking process.

5. Now add 500 ml of boiling water, watch out for the spluttering, add the fenugreek leaves and continue to boil for 5 minutes on high. Turn the heat down, put the lid on and simmer for 5 minutes.

Parveen's Top Tip

To enhance the flavour gently rub the dried fenugreek leaves in-between your palms, this releases some of the oils. The curry sauce is full of flavour even though it's actually quite runny, I serve it in a deep bowl which makes it easy to dip your naan bread in.

Chicken Jalfrezi

*T*his is my version of a Chicken Jalfrezi, it's made with red peppers and spring onions, it has a lighter, fresher flavour than a chicken masala but is equally as tasty. There are many different recipes, but I think when you have cooked this you will want to add it to your repertoire of dinner party favourites.

PREPARATION TIME: 10 MINUTES   COOKING TIME: 40 MINUTES   SERVES APPROX 6—8

Ingredients

3 medium sized chicken fillets — cut into 3 cm pieces

2 medium sized onions — finely sliced

1 tin chopped tomatoes — 400 g

2 red peppers — cut into 2 cm cubes

6 cloves of garlic — crushed or grated

2 cm fresh root ginger — grated

6 tbsp of vegetable oil

3 tbsp of chopped fresh coriander

1 bunch of spring onions — cut into 1 cm pieces

2 tsp of chilli powder

2 tsp of garam masala

1 tsp tandoori powder

¼ tsp turmeric powder

2 tsp salt

Method

1. Use a large pan with a lid, fry the onions in the oil until they are a golden brown. On medium heat, add ginger & garlic. Stir in and cook through for 1 minute.

2. Add chilli powder, garam masala, tandoori powder, turmeric powder and salt, stir fry for 1 minute, add a dash of water to cool down the cooking process.

3. Add the tomatoes and cook on medium heat for 10 minutes, keep stirring, if sauce sticks, add a dash of water. Cook until tomatoes have broken down.

4. Add chicken pieces, turn heat on high and continue stirring for 10 minutes. If sauce sticks, add a dash of water. Do not leave at this point; just keep stirring on high heat.

5. Add the red pepper and spring onions, cook for 2 minutes, these don't need too much cooking as we want to keep their shape.

6. Finally, add 200 ml of boiling water and fresh coriander, stir through & simmer for 10 minutes. This allows time for all the different flavours to infuse.

Parveen's Top Tip

Again, as with most of my chicken recipes you can try this dish with thigh and/or drumsticks, just remember to add a further 5 to 10 mins at step 6 if you are cooking with meat on the bone.

Chicken with Spinach

This is another combination of meat and vegetables that is a marriage made in heaven in my opinion. Again you can use most parts of the chicken, whether it's thigh, breast, drumsticks or the whole chicken cut into pieces. The only thing I really do insist on is that you need to use fresh spinach. These days you can buy ready to use, washed spinach in most supermarkets.

PREPARATION TIME: 10 MINUTES   COOKING TIME: 40 MINUTES   SERVES APPROX 6—8

Ingredients

3 medium sized chicken fillets — cut into 3 cm pieces

2 medium sized onions — finely diced

4 large fresh tomatoes — sliced

6 cloves of garlic — crushed or grated

500 g fresh spinach — finely chopped

2 cm fresh root ginger — grated

6 tbsp of vegetable oil

6 tbsp of fresh coriander

4 tsp dried fenugreek leaves

2 tsp chilli flakes

2 tsp garam masala

2 tsp salt

Method

1. Use a large pan with a lid, add the oil and fry the onions until they are golden brown. Add ginger and garlic and cook on medium heat for 1 to 2 minutes.

2. Add the chilli flakes, garam masala and salt, stir fry for 1 minute, add fresh tomatoes and cook on medium heat for 10 minutes. Keep stirring until tomatoes have broken down. If sauce sticks, add a dash of water.

3. Add chicken pieces, turn heat on high and stir fry for 5 minutes, ensuring that the chicken is totally covered in the lovely curry sauce.

4. Now keep heat on high and add the spinach, a handful at a time, allowing the spinach to wilt in between each handful.

5. You will notice quite a lot of water coming from the spinach, just keep stirring on high for 10 minutes and the water will just slowly disappear as the spinach cooks.

6. Add the fresh coriander and fenugreek leaves. Stir through for 2 minutes, cover with lid and simmer for a further 5 minutes, allowing all the leaves to infuse with the chicken.

Parveen's Top Tip

Although this recipe calls for fresh spinach you will be forgiven if you want to use frozen. The chicken will flavour the spinach, so if you want to cheat a little go ahead, just remember to cook out all the water. For extra flavour add 2 chopped tablespoons of fresh dill. It adds a different dimension to the dish, I love the flavour.

Chicken with Cauliflower and Potatoes

*O*ne thing that many Kashmiri style dishes do is to combine meat with vegetables. Some combinations work better than others. Sometimes I will cook curries like this, my boys will eat the meaty bits and I just eat the vegetables as I'm not a massive meat eater and oh yes, I usually add potatoes. I just love potatoes in any form and in this dish they take on the flavour of both the chicken and cauliflower.

PREPARATION TIME: 15 MINUTES   COOKING TIME: 40 MINUTES   SERVES APPROX 6—8

Ingredients

750 g of chicken thigh and breast — cut into 3 cm pieces

1 whole cauliflower — cut into small florets

6 new potatoes — halved

2 medium sized onions — thinly sliced

1 tin chopped tomatoes — 400 g

6 cloves of garlic — crushed

5 tbsp of vegetable oil

2 cm fresh root ginger — grated

3 tbsp of fresh coriander

1 tsp mild chilli powder

2 tsp of garam masala

¼ tsp turmeric powder

2 tsp salt

Method

1. Heat the oil in a large pan (use one with a lid) and add onions. Fry the onions until they are a golden brown. On medium heat, add ginger and garlic. Stir in and cook through for 1 minute.

2. Add chilli powder, turmeric, garam masala and salt, cook for 1 minute. Then add the tomatoes and cook on medium heat for 10 minutes, keep stirring, if the sauce sticks, add a dash of water.

3. Add chicken pieces, turn heat up to high and continue stirring for 10 minutes. Do not leave at this point; just keep stirring on high heat.

4. Add the potatoes and cauliflower, it will seem like there is not enough curry sauce to cover all the pieces of vegetable, but persevere and cook by stirring on high heat for 10 minutes, stirring every now and again.

5. Now add 100 ml of boiling water and the coriander, stir through, then with the lid on simmer on very low heat for 10 minutes.

Lamb Bhuna

This popular Kashmiri style curry is a must have at Asian Weddings. It's cooked en mass in huge pots and stirred using specially designed gigantic stirring shovels, for the want of a better word. Well, we Asians do tend to go OTT at Weddings and we usually have an average of 500 guests — and they ALL expect good food. The specially trained chefs use their own blend of garam masala plus a whole lot of whole spices. You can create the same flavours with this hassle-free recipe, just chuck it all in a pan and cook through!

PREPARATION TIME: 10 MINUTES   COOKING TIME: 1 HOUR   SERVES APPROX 4—6

Ingredients

900 g lamb diced into 2 cm cubes

2 medium sized onions — thinly sliced

3 tsp garam masala

1 tsp coriander powder

2 tsp chilli powder

¼ tsp turmeric powder

6 cloves of garlic — crushed

2 cm cube root ginger — crushed

2 tsp salt

1 tin of chopped tomatoes — 400 g

6 tbsp vegetable oil

2 tbsp fresh chopped coriander

Method

1. Wash meat and add all ingredients (except the coriander) into a large stock pot.

2. Bring to the boil and simmer for 30 minutes on low heat.

3. Turn the heat up to medium and cook the sauce for 10 minutes, stirring occasionally.

4. The meat and sauce will now have a shiny appearance with the oil separating. Stir continuously for 10 minutes. If sauce sticks, add a splash of water.

5. Add the coriander and 200 ml of boiling water, stir and simmer for 10 minutes or until tender.

Parveen's Top Tip

For best results, try and make your own garam masala, just follow my recipe on page 12. Also if you have sweet vine tomatoes, try chopping them instead of using tinned for a fresher taste.

Lamb Masala with Potatoes

This traditional lamb curry has a strong flavour and was one of my dad's favourite curries. Every time I would cook this, mum would tell me the same story about my dad coming home on leave from the Army (he was in the British Army in India). She said that he loved it so much and she made it so nice that he would polish off the whole lot in one go. My dad loved his food and it showed. I remember as a child he seemed so big; he was a larger than life character, in demeanour as well as in stature. I miss him but fondly remember his nickname for me "Little Chilli" how apt, given that I cook spicy food for a living.

PREPARATION TIME: 10 MINUTES   COOKING TIME: 1 HOUR & 20 MINUTES   SERVES APPROX 4—6

Ingredients

900 g lamb diced into 2 cm cubes

2 medium sized onions — thinly sliced

3 tsp garam masala

1 tsp coriander powder

1 tsp chilli powder

¼ tsp turmeric powder

6 cloves of garlic — crushed

2 cm cube root ginger — grated

2 tsp salt

1 tin of chopped tomatoes — 400 g

6 new potatoes — quartered

8 tbsp vegetable oil

2 tbsp fresh chopped coriander

Method

1. In a large stainless steel pan with a lid, add all ingredients (except the potatoes and coriander).

2. Bring to the boil and simmer for 20 minutes on low heat.

3. Turn the heat up to medium and cook for 20 minutes, stirring occasionally.

4. The lamb will now have a shiny appearance with the oil separating. Stir continuously for 15 minutes. If sauce sticks, add a splash of water.

5. Add the potatoes and stir in for 3 minutes on high heat, making sure the potatoes are evenly covered with the curry sauce.

6. Add the coriander and stir through, now add 200 ml of boiling water. With the lid on simmer for 20 minutes or until meat is tender and potatoes are cooked through.

Parveen's Top Tip

If you like your meat really tender, simmer for an extra 10 to 15 minutes. Although this recipe calls for boneless meat, if you ask your butcher for meat on the bone it will really enhance the flavour of the sauce or try this recipes with lamb chops — they taste amazing!

Lamb With Spinach

This is another perfect combination of meat with a vegetable. Just like the chicken with spinach it works so well together. You can make this recipe using lamb on the bone, it adds more flavour. In fact when my mum used to cook this she would ONLY cook it with meat on the bone, as a matter of fact — the bonier the better.

PREPARATION TIME: 20 MINUTES   COOKING TIME: 1 HOUR   SERVES APPROX 4—6

Ingredients

900 g lamb diced into 2 cm cubes

2 medium sized onions — thinly sliced

500 g fresh spinach — finely chopped

3 tsp garam masala

2 tsp chilli powder

3 tsp of dried fenugreek leaves

¼ tsp turmeric powder

6 cloves of garlic — crushed

2 cm cube root ginger — grated

1 tin of chopped tomatoes — 400 g

8 tbsp vegetable oil

2 tbsp fresh chopped coriander

2 tsp salt

Method

1. Into a large pan (with a lid) add the lamb, onions, ginger, garlic, tomatoes, turmeric, garam masala, salt and chilli powder, bring to the boil then simmer for 25 minutes on low heat.

2. Turn the heat up to medium, add the oil and cook for 10 minutes, stirring occasionally, if the sauce sticks, add a splash of water.

3. Turn heat to high and add the spinach, a handful at a time, allowing the spinach to wilt in between each handful. You will notice that the spinach will release water, just keep stirring on high for 10 minutes and the water just slowly reduces.

4. Add the fresh coriander and dried fenugreek leaves. Stir through and cook for a further 5 minutes on a medium heat allowing all the different flavours to infuse.

5. Finally, cover with lid and simmer for a further 10 minutes till the meat is tender or to your liking.

Parveen's Top Tip

This recipe always works really well with mutton, use shoulder or leg but just remember to add another 50 minutes to step 1. As with many of my amalgamations of meat and vegetables, I like to add potatoes to this recipe. Just add them at step 3, after you have added the spinach.

Mutton (on the bone) with Yellow Lentils

Mutton may take twice as long to cook than Lamb but in my opinion it tastes twice as good, so the extra time is well worth it. Again I have married two main ingredients to make one dish. This time it is a lentil and red meat. Many of my Asian friends make this for their families, it's not a dish that I have ever eaten in a restaurant but have had it many times growing up. I used to cook this when my mum came to visit as it was one of her favourites especially with her signature paratha.

PREPARATION TIME: 10 MINUTES   COOKING TIME: 2 HOURS   SERVES APPROX 4—6

Ingredients

900 g mutton on the bone, cut into 2 cm pieces

100 g of yellow lentils (channa daal)

2 medium sized onions — thinly sliced

3 tsp garam masala

1 tsp coriander powder

2 tsp chilli powder

¼ tsp turmeric powder

1 tin of chopped tomatoes — 400 g

6 cloves of garlic — crushed

2 cm cube root ginger — grated

2 tsp salt

8 tbsp vegetable oil

2 tbsp fresh chopped coriander

Method

1. Wash lentils several times and soak in a pan for an hour.

2. Into a large pan (with a lid) add the oil, mutton, onions, ginger, garlic, garam masala, salt, chilli powder, tomatoes, turmeric powder, coriander powder and 200 ml of water. Bring to the boil and simmer for 1 hour with lid on.

3. Now take the lid off, you will notice that the water has mostly evaporated and the meat and sauce have a shiny appearance with the oil separating. On high heat, cook the meat for 10 minutes, stirring to ensure that the sauce does not stick, if it does, add a splash of water.

4. Add the drained lentils and keeping the heat on high, stir occasionally for 10 minutes. Ensure that the lentils are covered with the lovely meaty sauce.

5. Pour in 300 ml of boiling water, add the coriander and boil on high for 5 minutes. Then cover with the lid and simmer for 30 to 40 minutes or until the lentils are cooked.

Parveen's Top Tip

For added flavour and texture my mum used to add 1 sliced onion into the curry at the same time as the coriander. The onions keep their shape and taste spicy but sweet. I find that chopped spring onions do the same job but just look a tad prettier.

Lamb with Okra (Ladies Fingers)

I know that okra is an acquired taste but if you do like it... which I do, try adding it to lamb. This dish is quite dry and has very little sauce. As we know, okra doesn't take kindly to getting wet (see my recipe for okra for the tale). Again this meat and vegetable dish has the best of both worlds, great tasting meat and flavoursome veg. I have made this several times for my clients and it is always well received. Serve with either chappattis or parathas.

PREPARATION TIME: 10 MINUTES	COOKING TIME: 1 HOUR	SERVES APPROX 4—6

Ingredients

900 g lamb diced into 2 cm cubes

2 medium sized onions — thinly sliced

300 g okra

3 tsp garam masala

1 tsp coriander powder

2 tsp chilli powder

¼ tsp turmeric powder

6 cloves of garlic — crushed

2 cm cube root ginger — grated

1 tin of chopped tomatoes — 400 g

6 tbsp vegetable oil

2 tbsp fresh chopped coriander

2 tsp salt

Method

1. Wash the okra whilst whole. Drain thoroughly, then wipe individual pieces with kitchen paper, ensuring that they are as dry as possible. Trim, top and bottom, then cut each okra into approx 2 cm pieces.

2. Heat 2 tbsp of oil in a frying pan, add the okra and stir fry for 5 minutes on high heat. They should crisp up slightly, drain and set aside. Discard the used oil.

3. Add all the rest of the ingredients (except the fresh coriander & okra) into a large pan, bring to the boil and simmer for 30 minutes on low heat.

4. The meat and sauce should now have a shiny appearance with the oil separating. Stir continuously for 10 minutes. If sauce sticks, add a splash of water. But keep stirring, do not be tempted to leave at this point.

5. Add the okra and gently stir for 5 minutes, be careful not to break apart the pieces of okra.

6. Add coriander, cover with lid and simmer for 10 minutes or until the lamb is cooked to your liking or tenderness.

Parveen's Top Tip

For added flavour, try adding extra onions at step 6. Just slice one small onion and add to the pan. I usually like to add red onion as I like the beautiful purple colour it adds to the dish.

Minced Lamb Curry (Keema Aloo Mattar)

When I cook Keema, it always reminds me of my handsome big brother. He is no longer with us but lives in our hearts. Keema was his absolute favourite curry, I would go as far as to say he was a bit obsessed with it. I remember as a young girl overhearing the conversations he used to have with my mum. He loved Keema that much that he used to say that the only criteria he had for the girl he marries is that she should be able to cook Keema like my mum. And he did, she could. Now, all these years later, it's actually my youngest son's favourite dish, in fact I use it as bribery. If I need him to help out around the house and he needs encouragement, I promise to make him Keema... it works every time!

PREPARATION TIME: 10 MINUTES   COOKING TIME: 1 HOUR   SERVES APPROX 4—6

Ingredients

900 g lamb mince

2 medium sized onions — thinly sliced

2 medium sized potatoes — peeled and quartered

200 g frozen peas

6 cloves of garlic — crushed

2 cm cube of root ginger — grated

1 tsp chilli powder

3 tsp garam masala

1 tsp coriander powder

¼ tsp turmeric powder

1 tin of chopped tomatoes — 400 g

6 tbsp vegetable oil

3 tbsp of fresh chopped coriander

2 tsp salt

Method

1. Into a large pan (with a lid) add the mince, onions, ginger, garlic, tomatoes, garam masala, coriander powder, turmeric powder, salt, chilli powder and oil. Bring to the boil then simmer for 20 minutes on low heat.

2. Turn the heat up to medium and cook for 20 minutes, stirring occasionally. The tomatoes and onions will have broken down, the oil will have separated from meat and risen to the surface.

3. Add the potatoes and cook on medium heat for 10 mins, stir occasionally.

4. Add the peas and stir fry the lamb mince for 2 – 3 minutes on high heat.

5. Finally, add the coriander and 50 ml of hot water, bring to boil, cover with lid and simmer for 5 minutes or until the potatoes are cooked.

Parveen's Top Tip

I often use mutton mince, it may be difficult to get hold of but most butchers will make it for you, if you ask. In fact my husband prefers the stronger flavour that mutton offers, which is quite good really, as it is almost half the price of lamb. So you get twice the flavour for half the price. Also, for extra flavour, try adding fresh fenugreek leaves, they have an earthier taste and work really well in the mince.

Vegetable Dishes

I think Indian food lends itself so well to vegetarianism and veganism. There are a huge variety of recipes for vegetables, pulses and lentils that I could have written for you, but I have chosen the most popular based on all my years of teaching Indian cookery. Once you have mastered these you can go onto experiment with other vegetables and legumes.

The method for many of the recipes is similar, i.e. make a masala sauce, add vegetables and cook through. You will notice that very little ginger, garlic and garam masala is used in this section, this is because I personally like to taste the actual vegetables without heavy spices. However, there is one particular ethnic herb I like to use a lot in my vegetarian dishes and that's dry fenugreek leaves (Methi). It has a really strong aroma and really enhances the flavour of most vegetables.

You can either buy your own spices or buy a spice bag containing all the spices highlighted in red from my website:

www.the-spicequeen.com

Tarka Daal

This mildly garlic flavoured, healthy lentil recipe is one of my most popular dishes. I have cooked it for almost every single dinner party I have ever catered. It's a firm favourite of my vegetarian and vegan clients, friends and family but is equally loved by meat eaters. Daal is a perfect accompaniment for both pilau rice and naan bread. I love it so much and I sometimes just have it as a soup. You can also adapt this recipe to suit your own palate. Try adding chick peas, spinach or even kale.

PREPARATION TIME: 10 MINUTES   COOKING TIME: 55 MINUTES   SERVES APPROX 4—6

Ingredients

250 g red split lentils

1 tsp salt

1 tsp chilli powder

½ tsp turmeric powder

2 tsp dried fenugreek leaves

2 medium sized onions — thinly sliced

4 tbsp vegetable oil

4 cloves of garlic — crushed

2 tbsp freshly chopped coriander

Method

1. Wash the lentils using cool water, 2 or 3 times, this washes out the starch and then drain.

2. Put the lentils in a large pan. Add 850 ml of hot water, salt, fenugreek leaves, turmeric & chilli. Bring to the boil, cover & simmer for 30 minutes, stirring occasionally.

3. The lentils should look like a thick soup now. If it's too thick, add a little hot water, and if it is too runny turn the heat up and cook on high for a few minutes. Remove from heat & set aside.

4. In a separate frying pan, on high heat, fry the onions until golden brown.

5. Add the crushed garlic & keep stirring on low heat for 5 minutes until onions and garlic have fused together. This is called the "tarka".

6. Gently add the "tarka" sauce to the cooked lentils, bring to the boil, add the coriander and stir through. Cover with lid & simmer for 10 minutes.

Parveen's Top Tip

If you want to add any chick peas, spinach or kale, add it at step 6 and follow the recipe through. And, if you are feeling in a decadent mood add a couple of tablespoons of butter. You can also use any variety of pulses and lentils with the recipe, from chick pea daal, green lentils and moong daal. My recipes are cooked with garlic and onions but if you are not a fan of garlic, try infusing it with ginger, many of my friends do and if you love garlic, try it with just a garlic infusion. Tarka daal can also be infused with just onions, sometimes my mum would make her Tarka Daal with an onion infusion and it would taste delicious but then again, everything mum cooked tasted good.

Saag Aloo

This "garlicky" light flavoured dish requires mostly fresh ingredients. When my mother cooked this, she always used fresh green chillies and not the dried red powdered chilli. The taste difference is subtle but noticeable. Many of my friends have only ever had the restaurant or takeaway version and are surprised when they have cooked my version and it exceeds all their expectations as all the fresh herbs really enhance the flavour of the spinach.

PREPARATION TIME: 15 MINUTES   COOKING TIME: 50 MINUTES   SERVES APPROX 4—6

Ingredients

500 g of fresh spinach — thoroughly washed and chopped

2 medium sized onions — thinly sliced

6 cloves of garlic — crushed

2 green chillies — very finely chopped or crushed

1 medium sized potato — diced into 1cm cubes

2 fresh tomatoes — finely chopped

6 tbsp vegetable oil

4 tbsp of freshly chopped coriander

3 tbsp of dried fenugreek leaves

1 tsp coriander seed powder

1 tsp salt

Method

1. Heat the oil in the pan and add onions. Fry the onions until they are a lightly golden brown.

2. On medium heat, add the garlic and chillies. Stir in and cook for 2 minutes.

3. Add tomatoes and salt, cook for 5 minutes or until tomatoes break down, keep stirring, if sauce sticks, add a splash of water.

4. Cover with lid and simmer for 5 minutes. Stir occasionally, allowing the onions and garlic to infuse.

5. Add potatoes and cook on high heat, making sure that all the potatoes are covered in the lovely garlic and chilli sauce.

6. Now add the spinach (a handful at a time) and stir in. The spinach will wilt very quickly. On high heat stir continuously for 10 minutes.

7. Add the coriander seed powder, fresh coriander and fenugreek leaves. Cover & simmer for 10 minutes or until potatoes are cooked.

Parveen's Top Tip

The spinach will produce a lot of water (step 6) make sure you cook this out otherwise it will taste "watery", if you wish to use frozen spinach you can, the taste is not as flavoursome but it's sometimes a good alternative if you can't get hold of any fresh spinach. Oh yes, for added flavour just add a knob of butter and salt when you add the coriander.

Spicy Eggs With Potatoes (Anday Aloo)

This simple egg dish is great to cook when you have no time and need a spice hit. There are so many different ways of making this recipe and I think each Asian family has their own take on it. We all have different versions, for example, my mum, my sister and I all have different ways of making "Anday Aloo" but they are equally as satisfying when hungry. I serve them with buttered chapattis but when I am feeling lazy I have them on toast.

PREPARATION TIME: 10 MINUTES   COOKING TIME: 10 MINUTES   SERVES APPROX 2—4

Ingredients

1 medium sized onion — thinly sliced

1 medium sized potato — peeled and thinly sliced

6 medium sized free range eggs

2 tomatoes — sliced or chopped

1 tsp chilli powder

½ tsp of chilli flakes (optional)

2 tsp of dried fenugreek leaves

1 tsp salt

4 tbsp vegetable oil

2 tbsp of chopped fresh coriander (stalks and leaves)

Method

1. In a frying pan add the oil and gently fry the sliced onions and potatoes for 5 minutes. The potatoes are thinly sliced so they should be cooked at the same time as the onions.

2. Add the sliced tomatoes, salt, chilli powder, chilli flakes and fenugreek leaves, cook by gently stirring with a wooden spoon for 5 minutes, the onions should be translucent and the potatoes nearly cooked.

3. In a bowl, beat the eggs and add the fresh coriander.

4. Pour the egg mixture into the pan and gently scramble for 2 to 3 minutes on medium heat. Keep stirring to make sure that the eggs are thoroughly cooked.

5. For added flavour sprinkle with fresh coriander leaves when serving.

Parveen's Top Tip

If you want to add a handful of spring onions when you add the coriander it will add to the taste as well as the texture. You can make this same recipe without potatoes, just add double the amount of onions, the dish tastes sweeter this way.

Aloo Mattar

*T*his vegetarian curry does not require many spices, in fact all you need is bit of chilli powder and a little coriander seed powder. It has a light flavour and is perfect served with plain boiled rice and cumin yoghurt. I find that when I have over indulged, this simple dish offers me respite from heavy foods. I usually make this curry when I don't have much in the house, as I will always have some potatoes and some frozen peas lying around in the freezer.

PREPARATION TIME: 5 MINUTES   COOKING TIME: 30 MINUTES   SERVES APPROX 4—6

Ingredients

2 medium sized onions — thinly sliced

200 g of frozen peas

3 medium sized potatoes, peeled and cut into 6 to 8 pieces

1 can of tinned chopped tomatoes (400 g) blitzed in a blender

1 tsp of chilli powder

1 tsp of coriander seed powder

½ tsp of fenugreek leaves (optional)

2 tsp salt

5 tbsp cooking oil

2 tbsp of chopped fresh coriander (stalks and leaves)

Method

1. Take a large pan (with a lid), add oil and sliced onions. Fry onions until golden brown on medium heat.

2. Add the blitzed tomatoes, salt, chilli powder, fenugreek leaves and coriander seed powder. Cook on high heat for 10 minutes until sauce is reduced to a thick consistency. Add a splash of water if the sauce sticks, then simmer with the lid on for 10 minutes.

3. You should now have a thick tomato based curry sauce, add the potatoes and some of the coriander stalks, cook on medium heat for 10 minutes, keep stirring, ensuring the potatoes are thoroughly covered with the curry sauce.

4. Add 300 ml of hot water and bring to the boil. Add the peas and boil on high for 2 to 3 mins.

5. Finally, add the rest of the fresh coriander, cover the pan and simmer on low for 2 to 3 mins or till the potatoes are cooked.

Parveen's Top Tip

If I need some extra protein I sometimes add hard boiled eggs, sliced in half lengthways. Also, this curry can be made as a drier dish like a masala. For those of you who like paneer you can adapt this quite easily. Just add paneer at stage 3 instead of potatoes.

Bindi (Ladies Fingers or Okra) with Potatoes

I first made this under my mother's instructions when I was 15. She wanted me to learn to cook the summer before my "O" Levels (yes, I am that old, now called GCSE's). Mum had told me when cooking vegetables to soak them after cutting, so that they didn't discolour. I had taken this on board; I cut the okra and dutifully soaked it. When it was time to take the okra pieces out of the water, I realised I had created an almighty messy gloop! It was a disaster. Even now when I cook okra, I can see the look of disdain on my mother's face. I may have come a long way from the under confident, gangly teenager with a monobrow; but every time I make okra, I think of my mum and smile to myself.

PREPARATION TIME: 10 MINUTES   COOKING TIME: 35 MINUTES   SERVES APPROX 4—6

Ingredients

500 g of okra (ladies fingers)

2 medium sized onions — halved & sliced

2 medium sized white potatoes — cut into 1 cm cubes

3 tomatoes — diced

1 tsp chilli powder

1 tsp dry fenugreek leaves

2 tbsp of fresh coriander (optional)

2 tsp salt

4 tbsp vegetable oil

Method

1. Wash the okra whilst whole. Drain thoroughly, then wipe each individual okra with kitchen paper ensuring that they are as dry as possible. Trim, top and bottom, then cut each okra into approx 2 cm pieces.

2. Heat 2 tbsp of oil in a frying pan, add the okra and stir fry for 5 minutes on high heat. They should crisp up slightly, drain and set aside. Discard the used oil.

3. In a separate non-stick pan, fry the onions and potatoes on high for 5 minutes, then add the tomatoes, chilli powder, fenugreek leaves, salt and cook for further 5 minutes and stir periodically.

4. Add the okra and stir all the ingredients together for 2 — 3 minutes.

5. Add the fresh coriander, cover with a lid and simmer for another 2 — 3 minutes. The potatoes should be soft and the okra should have kept its shape.

Parveen's Top Tip

No water should be used in the this style of cooking of okra, you don't want to make the mistake I made when first cooking it. Water will make the okra "slimy" but there are some cultures that prefer their okra that way. For added flavour and colour, I sometimes dice a red pepper and add to the dish at step 3.

Mixed Vegetable Curry

My version of a mixed vegetable curry only has three main vegetables, and they work so well in harmony. The aubergines add a creaminess, the red peppers look beautiful with their vibrant red colour and the spring onions give a "freshness" to the dish. Some recipes contain other vegetables such as cauliflower but I think that cauliflower can overpower the other flavours. My favourite part of cooking this recipe is emptying the contents into a serving dish and then cleaning out the hot pan with a bit of naan bread.

PREPARATION TIME: 15 MINUTES   COOKING TIME: 50 MINUTES   SERVES APPROX 4—6

Ingredients

2 medium sized onions — thinly sliced

2 peppers (red or green) — cut into 2 cm cubes

2 courgettes — sliced into semi circles

3 small aubergines — cut into 1 cm circular slices

1 tsp of chilli powder

1 tsp of cumin powder

2 tsp of fenugreek leaves

110 g of fresh or frozen peas

1 can of tinned tomatoes (chopped) — 400 g

2 tsp salt

5 tbsp vegetable oil

Method

1. Take a large pan (use pan with a lid), pour in oil and add sliced onions. Fry onions until golden brown.

2. Add a splash of water, so that onions don't burn. You should now have a brown looking onion sauce. Add the chilli powder, cumin powder and salt, cook on medium heat for 1 — 2 minutes.

3. Add the chopped tomatoes, cook for 10 minutes until sauce is reduced to a thick consistency, keep stirring, add a little bit of water if the curry sauce sticks to the bottom of the pan.

4. As the sauce reduces, the oil should come to the top. You now have a curry sauce base in which to cook your vegetables.

5. Add the courgettes and aubergines, cook on high heat for 10 minutes, keep stirring. You will notice that the vegetables will release water, but as you keep cooking, the water will dry out.

6. Add the red peppers and cook for 5 minutes, and keep stirring. Add the peas, fenugreek leaves and cook on medium to high heat for 3 — 4 minutes, allowing all the vegetables to mix in well. Cover the pan and simmer on low for 5 minutes.

Parveen's Top Tip

The more red peppers you have, the sweeter the dish will be. However the more green peppers you have in the dish the more bitter the curry will taste. Each to their own but personally I recommend using lots of red peppers, plus they look pretty when served. If you can't get a hold of fresh use frozen, it works quite well but at stage 5 cook out the extra water for about 5 minutes.

Mixed Pepper And Potato Masala

This is one of my daughter's favourite dishes. In her teenage years, she went through a vegetarian phase... which was just after her goth phase. I used to make this dish for her at least twice a week when she came home on holidays from University, I would make a special effort and cook it for her. She loved it so much that I would always make a little extra so she could pack it up into little plastic containers to take back with her. Her favourite way of eating it is on top of spaghetti with a little cheese, not very Asian I know — more Indo-Italian, well we are a multicultural society after all.

PREPARATION TIME: 5 MINUTES	COOKING TIME: 35 MINUTES	SERVES APPROX 4—6

Ingredients

2 medium sized onions — thinly sliced

3 medium sized potatoes — peeled and cut into 3 cm cubes

2 bell peppers, red, yellow or green — cut into 2 cm pieces

1 can of tinned chopped tomatoes — 400 g

1 tsp of chilli powder

1 tsp cumin powder

2 tsp of dried fenugreek leaves

2 tsp salt

1 bunch of spring onions — roughly chopped

5 tbsp vegetable oil

3 tbsp freshly chopped coriander

Method

1. Take a medium sized pan (with a lid), add oil and sliced onions. Fry onions until golden brown on medium heat.

2. Add the chopped tomatoes, salt, chilli powder, cumin powder and dried fenugreek leaves. Cook on high heat for 10 minutes until sauce is reduced to a thick consistency. Add a splash of water if the sauce sticks.

3. You should now have a thick tomato based curry sauce. Add the potatoes, cook on medium heat for 5 minutes and keep stirring. The potatoes may stick due to the starch, if they do just add a splash of water and keep stirring.

4. Now add the mixed peppers, on high heat, keep stirring for about 5 minutes making sure that all the sauce has completely covered the potatoes and peppers.

5. Finally, add the spring onions, fresh coriander and 100 ml of water, cover with lid and simmer for 10 minutes or till the potatoes are cooked.

Parveen's Top Tip

You can use any colour of peppers but I like to use as many different colours as I can possibly get a hold of. But don't worry too much just use what you have. Also, I sometimes leave some of the seeds in, they are not hot but look quite attractive in the finished dish.

Bombay Potatoes

You can use this recipe to make bombay potatoes as it requires the same spice and the same method. To make bombay potatotes, just substitute the bell peppers with 2 medium sized potatoes at stage 3 and cook for 10 minutes. Leave out step 4 and follow step 5 until potatoes are cooked through. There are many different methods of making bombay potatoes, I like this one as it has a little bit of a masala sauce.

Chana Masala (Chick Pea) with Spring Onions

This fantastic tasting vegetarian curry is surprisingly quite filling for a non-meat dish. When I make it for family dinner parties even the carnivores will have a second helping. And I know my recipe hits the right spot as even my brother-in-law loves my chick pea masala and he is notoriously difficult to please, mostly because my big sister is a wonderful cook. It must run in the family!

PREPARATION TIME: 10 MINUTES   COOKING TIME: 50 MINUTES   SERVES APPROX 4—6 (WITH RICE)

Ingredients

2 medium sized onions — thinly sliced

2 tins of chick peas — washed & drained

1 tin chopped tomatoes (400 g) — blitzed in blender

4 cloves of garlic — crushed

1 tsp chilli powder

1 tsp of coriander powder

2 tsp of salt

6 tbsp vegetable oil

5 spring onions chopped

Method

1. Heat the oil in the pan and add onions. Fry the onions until they are a golden brown.

2. On medium heat, add garlic, stir in and cook through for 1 minute.

3. Add tomatoes, chilli powder, salt, coriander powder and cook on medium heat for 10 minutes, keep stirring, if sauce sticks, add a dash of water. The oil will separate and the sauce should have a thick consistency now.

4. Simmer on lowest heat for 10 minutes, this allows all the flavours to infuse.

5. Add chick peas, stir well, make sure that all the chick peas are covered in the sauce. Turn heat up to high and continue stirring for 5 to 7 minutes. If sauce sticks, add a dash of water and continue to stir.

6. Add 100 ml of boiling water, stir through, add fresh coriander and spring onions. With lid on, simmer for 5 minutes. This is just enough time for the spring onions and coriander to flavour the chickpeas.

Parveen's Top Tip

You can use this recipe to cook several types of beans and pulses. You don't have to use fresh beans, tinned will taste just as good. I often make the same recipes with butter beans or black eyed beans. Sometimes with tinned beans one can taste the "tinny, metallic" taste but the masala sauce has such a strong flavour that once you have cooked the beans, they will have ingested all those lovely spices and taste great.

"I love Gobi with Naan, a cucumber Raita and lemon and coriander salad.
Try it for yourself. "

Aloo Gobi

I love this flavoursome vegetarian dish, especially with freshly made hot chapattis. The first time I made it for my husband, over 2 decades ago, he was not impressed and I was not happy. I had cooked it so much that all the cauliflower florets broke down into a sort of mush — a bit like my pride. So I tweaked the recipe to the way he likes it, with the florets slightly al dente and intact... pride restored!

PREPARATION TIME: 10 MINUTES	COOKING TIME: 35 MINUTES	SERVES APPROX 4—6

Ingredients

2 medium sized onions — thinly sliced

1 whole cauliflower cut into florets

3 medium sized potatoes — cut into 3 cm cubes

1 can of tinned chopped tomatoes — 400 g

2 tsp of dried fenugreek leaves

2 tsp coriander powder (optional)

1 tsp chilli powder

½ tsp cumin powder

2 tsp salt

6 tbsp vegetable oil

Method

1. Take a large stainless steel pan (use pan with a lid) add oil and sliced onions. Fry the onions until they are golden brown. Add a splash of water, so that onions don't burn. You will now have a brown looking onion sauce.

2. Add the chopped tomatoes, chilli powder, cumin powder, coriander powder, salt and cook for 10 minutes until sauce is reduced to a thick consistency (keep stirring, add a little water if the curry sauce sticks to the bottom of the pan).

3. Add the potatoes and on high heat cook for 5 minutes, keep stirring.

4. Now add the cauliflower and cook in the curry sauce for approx 10 minutes, keep stirring. Add a splash of water to avoid the sauce sticking.

5. Finally add fenugreek leaves, and 3 tbsp of water, cover the pan and simmer on low for 5 minutes or until cauliflower and potatoes are cooked.

Parveen's Top Tip

You can add the green leaves of the cauliflower for taste, or perhaps add a red bell pepper to the dish, it adds a different dimension to the taste and it's delicious! If you decide to use one of my spice bags, just add the whole bag at stage 2 and follow the rest of the recipe, although you won't need to add the fenugreek leaves at stage 5 as you will have already done that.

Rice Dishes

In my experience, most people would probably have never had an authentic pilau rice dish. Many Indian restaurants and takeaways serve a version of it, but it's a world away from the real thing. Traditional Kashmiri style rice is usually made in a stock, whether it's vegetable or meat. Traditional pilau rice is as flavoursome as a kedgeree and as filling as a risotto.

Before you reach for the "boil in the bag" rice, try some of these recipes and you will be pleasantly surprised at the depth of flavour and self satisfaction at having made it yourself; with not a bag in sight, well unless you count my little spice bags.

You can either buy your own spices or buy a spice bag containing all the spices highlighted in red from my website:

www.the-spicequeen.com

Pilau Rice with Peas & Potatoes

Reading the title, you may be forgiven for being a little confused, most recipes would be for rice OR potatoes, but with this traditional rice dish — we have both rice AND potatoes. The rice is not spicy but so flavoursome that it can even be eaten as a main meal with a cucumber raita and salad. Also, remember to use a large pan with a lid as rice almost doubles in size when cooked. Also for best results, use a basmati rice it makes all the difference.

PREPARATION TIME: 1 HOUR TO SOAK RICE   COOKING TIME: 50 MINUTES   SERVES APPROX 4—6 (WITH CURRY)

Ingredients

500 g of white basmati rice

1 medium sized onion — finely diced

200 g frozen peas

3 tsp garam masala

1 heaped tsp coarsely ground cumin

2 fresh tomatoes — diced

6 baby potatoes — halved

6 tbsp vegetable oil

2 green chillies — cut into 3 pieces

2 tsp salt

Brown Rice

You can use brown rice if you prefer, just add double the amount of water to rice and add an extra 10 minutes on the simmering time at step 6. And, if you are on a healthy eating plan, half the amount of oil. The rice will still taste good.

Method

1. Place rice in a large bowl. Gently wash through 4 times in cold water, this is to wash out most of the starch, so the rice does not stick together. Soak for an hour.

2. Add oil to a large pan and fry onions until they are very dark brown. Add 20 ml of water and immediately cover with the lid. Turn heat to low & leave the lid on for 1 minute.

3. Add the tomatoes, green chillies, garam masala, cumin and salt. Cook on medium heat for 5 – 10 minutes or until the tomatoes have broken down. Keep stirring, if the sauce sticks, add a splash of water.

4. You will now have a dark brown onion sauce. Add the potatoes and peas. Cook on medium heat for 5 minutes, stirring all the time.

5. Add 750 ml of boiling water, continue to boil for 2 minutes — this is your stock.

6. Add drained rice to the stock. Stir once & boil on high heat for 3 minutes. Gently stir once more and cover with the lid & leave to simmer on the lowest heat possible for 25 minutes. Do not be tempted to take a peek, just leave it alone & you will have perfectly cooked rice.

Parveen's Top Tip

The flavour & the colour of the rice is due to the way the onions are fried, so don't worry if they look a little charred. For added flavour, try adding 30 g of butter to the stock at step 5, I usually do. Although this recipe uses peas you can cook this same recipe with chick peas, just substitute the peas for 2 tins of chick peas.

Buttered Cumin Rice

*T*his rice dish does not require as much cooking as a pilau and has a little more flavour than plain boiled rice. I usually make it when I fancy some rice but have not got time to make a full-on pilau rice. This rice dish has a light flavour and a golden yellow colour due to the butter and cumin. To add a little texture and taste add a handful of frozen peas.

PREPARATION TIME: 1 HOUR	COOKING TIME: 30 MINUTES	SERVES APPROX 4—6

Ingredients

500 g white basmati rice

1 tsp salt

1 tsp coarse ground cumin

30 g butter

Method

1. Place rice in a large bowl. Gently wash through 4 to 5 times or until the water runs clear. Soak for an hour in cool or tepid water.

2. In a large pan (with a lid) add the oil and butter. Add the cumin and on high heat cook for 1 to 2 minutes.

3. Add 750 ml of hot water and the salt, bring to the boil and continue to boil for 2 minutes.

4. Turn heat down to the lowest possible heat, add the drained rice, cover pan with lid and simmer for 30 minutes. Leave the rice alone, do not take off the lid to check it as this interferes with the cooking process.

5. After 30 minutes take off the lid, the rice will have absorbed all the water and you should have long and lightly coloured golden grains of rice that separate easily with a fork.

Parveen's Top Tip

If you do not have time to soak the rice, just wash out the starch and add an extra 250 ml of water when boiling. As a general rule, double the amount of water to rice when NOT soaked, but when you have soaked it, use one and half times the water, as I have in this recipe.

Chicken Pilau Rice

*T*his rice dish is the one I make the most often when I have guests. It does not take as long as Biryani, which is hard work frankly, but I think has just as much flavour. I use chicken on the bone to make a wonderfully tasting chicken stock in which I then cook the rice. The rice takes on ALL the flavours of the chicken stock. It's a truly heart-warming satisfying rice dish. As with any of my rice dishes, it's best served with a cucumber raita.

PREPARATION TIME: 1 HOUR TO SOAK RICE   COOKING TIME: 1 HOUR   SERVES APPROX 6—8

Ingredients

500 g of white basmati rice

500 g chicken pieces — thigh, drumsticks or wings

2 medium sized onions — finely diced

3 tsp of garam masala

2 tsp cumin powder

2 fresh tomatoes — diced

6 tsp vegetable oil

2 green chillies — cut into 4 pieces

2 tsp salt

Method

1. Place the rice in a large bowl. Gently wash through 4 times in cold water, this is to wash out the excess starch so the rice does not stick together. Soak for an hour.

2. Add oil to a large pan and fry onions until they are very dark brown. Add 20 ml of water and immediately cover with the lid. Turn heat to low and leave the lid on for 1 minute.

3. Add the tomatoes, green chillies, garam masala, cumin and salt. Cook on medium heat for 5 minutes or until the tomatoes have broken down, if sauce sticks add a dash of water.

4. Add the chicken pieces and cook on high heat for 10 minutes, stirring all the time. The chicken will turn a brown colour as it takes on the colours of the dark brown onion sauce.

5. Add 750 ml of boiling water, continue to boil for 10 minutes — this is your chicken stock.

6. Add drained rice to the stock. Gently stir once and boil on high heat for 3 minutes. Gently stir once more, cover with the lid and leave to simmer on the lowest heat possible for 25 minutes.

Parveen's Top Tip

Sometimes to add even more textures and flavours, I will add other vegetables as well as the chicken. I often add a tin of chick peas or 100 g of frozen peas, just add the peas or chick peas after step 5. Or try adding some potatoes, it may be a carb overload but boy it tastes good.

Plain Boiled Rice

I think plain boiled rice is one of the easiest dishes to make but the hardest to get right. So I have written this simple recipe for people who just like to have plain boiled rice with their curries. But I will let you in on a little secret, mine does not always turn out perfect. There are so many factors to consider, the brand of the rice, the style of pan, and the type of hob. So please do not be disheartened if your rice does not turn out right — just keep practicing. The old cliché is true, practice makes perfect and I am 100% confident this recipe works 99% of the time.

PREPARATION TIME: 1 HOUR	COOKING TIME: 30 MINUTES	SERVES APPROX 4–6

Ingredients

500 g white basmati rice

1 tsp salt

1 tbsp vegetable oil

Method

1. Place rice in a large bowl. Gently wash through 4 to 5 times or until the water runs clear. The aim of the game is to wash out the starch so the rice does not clump together.

2. Soak the rice for an hour in tepid water, this will help the rice swell, so you will have beautiful long grains of rice for your finished dish.

3. Drain the rice and gently transfer to a large pan (with lid). Add 750 ml of water, salt and vegetable oil, bring to the boil and continue to boil for 2 to 3 minutes.

4. Turn heat down to the lowest possible, cover pan with lid and simmer for 25 minutes. Leave the rice alone, do not take off the lid to check it as this interferes with the cooking process.

5. Once it has simmered take off the lid, the rice will have absorbed all the water. You can fluff up with a fork if you wish.

Parveen's Top Tip

If you are feeling adventurous, you can fluff up the rice the way I do; firmly press the lid with a tea-towel, turn the pan upside down several times and shake it from side to side. The rice at the bottom should have moved to the top and vice versa.

Breads

I don't know about you, but I love my carbs. I love all the breads in this section but as a general rule, like most Asian mums, I make chapattis as a staple for my family. They are the perfect accompaniment to any curry or masala. Don't worry if you don't get round chapattis and naan's — just keep practicing. I may be able to make them with my eyes closed now, but it wasn't always like that, it took years of practice. I remember whilst mum was teaching me to make chapattis she would slap the back of my hand and say "if you don't make round chapattis, you'll never find a husband!". Well, little did she know that is not how I got my husband... but it's how I kept him.

You can either buy your own spices or buy a spice bag containing all the spices highlighted in red from my website:

www.the-spicequeen.com

Chapattis

Chapattis, also known as flatbread or roti are a staple in most Asian households. Just as potatoes are for the English, pasta for the Italians and noodles for the Chinese. Perhaps I am being a little stereotypical but you get the general idea. Chapattis have very little flavour as they contain no spice, salt or oils. But they work perfect in partnership with hot, spicy curries. You can cook them and reheat but I personally think there's nothing in the world that beats hot beautifully round chapattis straight off the pan. They are so addictive that one is never enough!

PREPARATION TIME: 5 MINUTES   COOKING TIME: 10 MINUTES   SERVES APPROX 8

Ingredients

450 g chapatti or wholewheat flour

250 ml water — (cold or tepid)

25 g butter for spreading — optional

Method

1. Place the flour in a deep bowl, slowly add the water and mix together. The flour will absorb all the water and the dough will be a little sticky at this point, cover and set aside. After 20 minutes, take the dough and knead for 2 minutes until it is smooth and soft. Place the dough in an airtight container and pop into the fridge for a further 20 minutes.

2. Now take the dough out of the fridge, divide into eight pieces and shape each piece into a ball (image 1). Flatten the balls slightly using your hands (image 2). With a rolling pin, roll into a flat disc approximately 15 cm—17 cm in diameter. As with rolling pastry, use the flour to stop the chapattis sticking to the surface.

3. Heat a frying pan or the chapatti pan (if you have one) till warm. Take the chapatti, place it on the palm of your hand, then transfer from one palm to another, in a clapping motion. Do this 5 or 6 times in quick succession. This helps to shake off the excess flour.

4. Lay the chapatti on the pan and cook for about 20—30 seconds or until the surface bubbles slightly (image 3).

5. Turn it over with tongs or using fingertips if you are brave enough (image 4). Cook the other side for 10 – 15 seconds. As soon as brown spots appear on the underside the chapatti is done. If the dough looks uncooked in areas, use a clean tea towel and gently press down on the areas that need extra cooking — this only take a few more seconds.

6. Repeat with the other seven balls using the remaining flour to roll them out. Stack them up as they are cooked and cover with a clean tea towel to keep them warm. Spread butter over one side for a more delicious taste, naughty but nice!

Parveen's Top Tip

The longer you knead the dough, the softer the chapattis are and remember it takes years of practice to make round, even chapattis, so persevere and keep practising. My first chapattis were all shapes, sizes and thickness but my dad, bless him, said they were perfect. That's love!

Paratha

A Paratha is a flatbread made of wheat flour with lashings of butter. There are so many ways to make them but this recipe is my mum's... it was her signature dish. Nobody could make parathas as good as her... believe me we have all tried! Even at the age of 50 when I had a long day ahead of me, mum used to rustle up a few parathas with sweet chai to fuel me up for the day and they did — they are very filling indeed.

PREPARATION TIME: 5 MINUTES	COOKING TIME: — 10 MINUTES	SERVES APPROX 4

Ingredients

500 g chapatti or plain flour

250 ml water — cold or tepid

250 g butter — cold

½ tsp of salt

Method

1. Place the flour and salt into a deep mixing bowl. Slowly add the water mixing together to make a dough. The dough will be a little sticky at this point. Cover with a cloth and set aside for 20 minutes.

2. Knead the dough for 2 minutes until it is smooth and soft. Store in an airtight container and keep at room temperature.

3. Divide the dough into eight equal portions and shape each one into a ball.

4. Two balls at a time, place onto a clean floured surface (image 1). Roll each ball to about 5 cm diameter (use the dry flour to stop the dough sticking to the surface). Using a knife, add 2 teaspoons of butter onto one of the 5 cm discs of dough (image 2). Place the other disc on top, pressing the edges together (image 3).

5. Heat a griddle or a shallow frying pan till warm, not hot as you will be cooking with butter and we do not want it to burn. Lay the paratha on the pan and cook for about 1 minute or until the surface bubbles slightly. Spread a teaspoon of butter onto the paratha and then turn it over with tongs or a fish slice (image 4). Add another teaspoon of butter on the surface as it cooks. Turn over one last time and cook for another 30 seconds.

6. Repeat steps 5 and 6 with the rest of the dough balls. Stack them as you are cooking them, separating each one either with tin foil or greaseproof paper.

Parveen's Top Tip

If you want to be a little healthier and not use as much butter, simply halve the amount but please do not be tempted to use half fat butter or margarine as these usually contain water and this will make the paratha "soggy" which we don't want, parathas are best when crispy and flaky.

Aloo Paratha

These are crispy, slightly salty Kashmiri flatbreads made with layers of buttery dough and stuffed with spiced potato. Aloo paratha is a meal in itself, extremely tasty and extremely filling. I remember when I was a child, mum would make a huge stack of aloo parathas and a flask of sweet chai when we were going on a family day trip to Blackpool. We would stop off for a picnic en route and eat our parathas and drink our chai out of plastic cups. It may sound very basic but it was a happy time. Even now when I make aloo paratha, I think of those happy day trips travelling up to Blackpool Pleasure Beach, in the back of dad's van listening to his old Indian classic songs.

PREPARATION TIME: 20 MINUTES　　　COOKING TIME: 20 MINUTES　　　SERVES APPROX 4

Ingredients

500 g chapatti flour or plain flour

250 ml tepid water

250 g butter — cold

½ tsp Salt

For the Filling:

6 medium sized potatoes — peeled and diced into 2 cm cubes

1 tbsp chopped coriander leaves

½ tsp cumin powder

1 tsp chilli flakes

1 tsp coriander powder

1 small onion — very finely diced

¼ tsp salt

Parveen's Top Tip

Remember you will only need about 2 minutes cooking time as the potatoes are already cooked, so you are just cooking the dough. Once you gain confidence with these you can experiment with the filling, you can add more spice, more or less onions — just tailor make it to suit your palate.

Method

1. In a deep bowl, add flour, salt, and slowly mix in the water using your hands to make the dough. Cover the bowl with a cloth and set aside for 20 minutes. Then knead the dough for 2 minutes or till smooth and soft. Place in an airtight container and store in the fridge.

2. To make the potato filling, boil the potatoes in salted water for 10 minutes. Drain the potatoes, add salt, chilli flakes, cumin powder, coriander powder, fresh coriander and onions. Roughly mash together using a fork and set aside.

3. Take the dough and divide into eight equal portions shaping each one into a ball. Place 2 onto a clean floured surface and roll out to approximately 8 cm diameter (use dry flour to stop the dough sticking to the surface). Spread a heaped tablespoon of the potato filling (Image 1) leaving a 1 cm edge. Place the other disc of dough on top, creating a potato sandwich (Image 2). Gently roll out the paratha to a diameter approx 13 cm.

4. Heat a non-stick shallow frying pan, till warm (use a chapatti pan, if you have one). Lay the paratha on the pan and cook for about 30 seconds. (Image 4). Spread a teaspoon of butter onto the paratha and then carefully turn it over with a fish slice. Spread another teaspoon of butter and cook for a further 30 seconds, turn over once more and cook for 30 seconds.

5. Place on a plate and cover with kitchen foil to keep warm. Clean the pan with a kitchen towel and repeat the process to make the other 3 parathas. Stack them as you are cooking them, separating each one with either tin foil or greaseproof paper.

Naan Bread

Contrary to popular belief, most Asian housewives rarely make naan at home, probably because one requires a traditional Tandoori oven and very few of us have one in the back garden! I just improvise and use my hob and oven heavily masquerading as a clay Tandoori oven. Well, I am nothing if not resourceful. With this recipe I have used baking powder but if you want to have a "fluffier" naan, then feel free to use yeast instead.

PREPARATION TIME: 1 TO 2 HOURS FOR DOUGH TO RISE   COOKING TIME: 5 TO 10 MINUTES   SERVES APPROX 6

Ingredients

250 g plain flour

2 tsp sugar

½ tsp salt

½ tsp baking powder

120 ml milk

2 tbsp vegetable oil

For the topping:

1 tsp softened butter

50 g sesame seeds

Method

1. In a large bowl, add sifted flour, sugar, salt, baking powder and mix together. Then in a jug mix together the milk and the oil.

2. Make a well in the centre of the flour mixture and slowly pour in the liquid mixture, whilst stirring with the wooden spoon, the flour will absorb all the liquid. Then knead well for 8—10 minutes to make a soft smooth dough, if the dough is too sticky just add a little flour as you are kneading it.

3. Place the dough into an oiled bowl, cover with a damp tea-towel and leave in a warm place for 10—15 minutes. The dough will have risen now, divide into six equal portions and form into dough balls.

4. On a clean floured surface, roll the dough balls into circles and quite thinly (3 to 4 mm) remember the naan will rise when cooked. If the dough sticks, use a little flour.

5. Use a non-stick frying pan and on a medium heat, place the naan in the pan and cook for 1—2 minutes, then carefully remove from pan and place on a baking tray under a hot grill, for 2 minutes or until golden brown — spread with a little butter and sesame seeds, serve hot.

Peshwari Naan

These sweet, fluffy, tasty naan are usually a favourite of my friends when we go out to eat at an Indian Restaurant. The sweetness of the almond and fruit works in perfect harmony with spicy main dishes. I must confess, I hardly make them at home but I thought it would be most unfair not to include them in the book as I know this is a firm favourite for a lot of you curry lovers out there. When I do make them I just eat them hot with a cup of tea, so satisfying.

PREPARATION TIME: 1 TO 2 HOURS	COOKING TIME: 5 TO 10 MINUTES	SERVES APPROX 6

Ingredients

350 g strong bread flour

7 g sachet easy-bake dried yeast

1 tsp salt

50 ml natural yoghurt

150 ml hand-hot water (approx)

20 ml vegetable oil

50 g butter

For filling:

25 g desiccated coconut

25 g flaked almonds

25 g sultanas or raisins (optional)

Method

1. Mix the flour, yeast and salt in a large bowl. Stir in the yoghurt and enough water to mix to a soft bread like dough. Knead on a lightly floured surface for 5 minutes until smooth and elastic.

2. Place the dough in a lightly oiled bowl and cover with a clean tea towel. Set aside in a warm place for about 1 ½ to 2 hrs or until the dough has doubled in size.

3. To make the filling: add the nuts and fruit into a food processor or blender and process to a coarse paste.

4. Preheat the oven to 220°C/Gas Mark 7. Take a baking tray, brush with a little oil and place it into the oven to heat up.

5. Divide the dough into 6 pieces, take one piece and roll out into a 5 cm circle. Sprinkle 1 tbsp of the filling into the centre of the naan, pull the edges together to enclose the filling creating a parcel shaped ball. Place onto a floured surface and roll out into a thin oval shape approx 3 to 4 mm in thickness.

6. Place the naan on the hot baking tray and bake for 7–8 minutes or until the naan puffs up and golden brown spots appear. Spread with a little butter and serve immediately whilst lovely and hot. Make 2 at a time for ease.

Parveen's Top Tip

If you want to make a batch and keep them, just make sure you wrap them in some kitchen foil and then place them in a plastic bag. They will keep in the fridge for 2 to 3 days with no compromise to the taste. To heat up just pop them in a warm frying pan for 30 seconds on each side.

Dips & Salads

I think that dips and salads are just as important as the spicy sensations that chillies deliver during an Indian meal. Think of this section of the book as a cooling system for your mouth. I personally wouldn't dream of having a meal without a little salad or yoghurt to counterbalance the heat of a curry. I quite enjoy cleansing my palate with a cooling cucumber raita, ready for the next mouth-watering mouthful.

You can either buy your own spices or buy a spice bag containing all the spices highlighted in red from my website:

www.the-spicequeen.com

Cucumber Raita

*T*his yoghurt sauce is traditionally always served with rice, in fact no Asian housewife worth her salt would dream of serving rice without a yoghurt raita. I remember as a child watching my mum make her own yoghurt, she would cultivate it with a spoon on previously made yoghurt in her trusted brown clay pot. She would leave it overnight on top of the pilot light of our gas cooker, a pilot light is a mini open flame in the middle of the cooker and the flame is as small as a candle. Modern day cookers are fitted with igniters, R.I.P. Pilot Light. I usually make a cucumber raita and leave it in my fridge so it's there when I need it. It will happily sit in the fridge for 2 to 3 days.

PREPARATION TIME: 5 MINUTES   COOKING TIME: —   SERVES APPROX 4—6

Ingredients

8 tbsp of natural or greek yoghurt

¼ small white onion

¼ cucumber

½ tsp salt

Method

1. In a small bowl, add the yoghurt and mix until smooth.

2. Dice the cucumber and onion into 5 mm cubes.

3. Add cucumber and onion into yoghurt.

4. Add the salt and mix together, store in the fridge or eat as required.

Parveen's Top Tip

If you want the coolness of yoghurt with your meal with no other bits added, just add a pinch of salt to natural yoghurt. That also works a treat with most curries and rice dishes.

Green Chilli and Mint Dip

This hot tasting mint and green chilli dip is the perfect accompaniment to onion bhajis, tandoori chicken, lamb sheesh kebabs, well basically 99% of my starters, in Punjabi this is called chutney. You can whiz it up in a blender but I will often make it in a mortar and pestle, I think it adds a certain flavour when made like this. Even though this green chilli dip contains fresh mint which is usually cooling, this dip packs quite a punch, predominantly due to the content of green chilli. I usually make it and have a pot of it in the fridge, so it is there when I need it. It will happily survive in the fridge for 4 or 5 days. I am not a huge fan as it's a little too hot for me but my husband just loves it... maybe even more than me.

PREPARATION TIME: 5 MINUTES   COOKING TIME: 2 MINUTES   SERVES APPROX 6—8

Ingredients

6 tbsp of natural yoghurt

2 tbsp of chopped fresh mint leaves

1 tbsp of fresh chopped coriander

3 green chillies — chopped

½ fresh tomato

½ tsp salt

1 tsp fresh lemon Juice

Method

1. In a blender, add the chopped mint leaves, coriander, green chillies, tomatoes and 2 tbsp of the yoghurt. Blend for 1 minute.

2. Empty the contents of the blender into a bowl and stir in the remainder of the yoghurt.

3. Add the salt and lemon juice.

4. Season to taste, store in fridge in a covered pot until you are ready to serve.

Quick Cheats Mint Dip

You can always make a cheat's version. Just add a level teaspoon of ordinary mint sauce and ¼ teaspoon of salt to 6 tablespoons of yoghurt and stir — easy!

Parveen's Top Tip

If you would like your dip hotter, just add 1 or 2 more green chillies and remember, serve the dip at room temperature, it tastes much better.

"I love the way that tamarind looks when swirled with yoghurt"

Tamarind Dipping Sauce

I absolutely love this sweet, sour and chilli dip. When I was expecting my daughter, Sherine, it's the first thing I used to eat every morning on top of chaat. Strangely, she is not a fan of it but I am. In fact I am sometimes accused by my husband of force feeding it to my guests with my famous chaat — well, I just want them to love it as much as I do. The process may seem quite lengthy but once made the sauce will last in the fridge for a week to 10 days, so if you pro-rata the time, it's only a minute a day.

PREPARATION TIME: -   COOKING TIME: 10 MINUTES   SERVES APPROX 4—6

Ingredients

Dried block of tamarind fruit — 200 g

400 ml water

¼ tsp salt

½ tsp of chilli flakes

Method

1. In a pan, add the tamarind fruit, 400 ml water and boil. You will find that as the water heats up, the solid fruit will start to breakdown. Using the back of a wooden spoon, break down the pieces of tamarind, once broken stir and boil on low for about 10 minutes.

2. Now strain the mixture into a small bowl using a sieve, you should be left with the stones and the pith of the tamarind fruit in the sieve.

3. Add salt and chilli flakes to the bowl and stir in.

4. Store in a jar with a lid and serve as needed.

Parveen's Top Tip

If I am really busy, I will sometimes buy a bottle of tamarind sauce from the Asian supermarket. If you buy a good quality bottled variety, the taste is surprisingly good. Recently, I noticed that several of my local supermarkets are also selling tamarind sauce. It may be cheating a little — well even though sometimes we all strive to be domestic goddesses and gods in the kitchen, we all need a day off.

Minty Dip

A fresh tasting minty yoghurt dip—the perfect accompaniment to onion bhajis, tandoori chicken, lamb sheesh kebabs, basically any starter. The mint is cooling, the yoghurt is cooling and it's a great palate cleanser. You will most probably have eaten it with popadoms in an Indian restaurant. It's so easy and so simple that once you have made it, you will make it time and time again.

PREPARATION TIME: 2 MINUTES	COOKING TIME: —	SERVES APPROX 6—6

Ingredients

6 tbsp of natural yoghurt

1 level tsp mint sauce

½ tsp of salt

Method

1. Using a small bowl, add the yoghurt, salt and mint.

2. Mix till smooth, (the consistency should be like double cream)

3. Eat as required or store the rest in an airtight container

Cumin Yoghurt

This salty yoghurt sauce calms down the palate when eating spicy food. I usually have it with a starter topped with tamarind sauce. I know that generally in the Western culture yoghurt is usually sweet but in Indian cuisine it's very commonplace to have yoghurt with a meal. I usually make a pot of cumin yoghurt and store it in the fridge. My youngest son loves it so much that if there is none in the fridge he will refuse to have a meal without it and just opt for a bowl of cereal instead, a poor substitute I know, well Cyrus is an all or nothing kind of guy.

PREPARATION TIME: 5 MINUTES	COOKING TIME: —	SERVES APPROX 4—6

Ingredients

6 tbsp plain or Greek yoghurt

2 tbsp of milk

¼ tsp of salt

Half a medium sized onion — diced (optional)

½ tsp coarsely ground cumin

Method

1. Using a small bowl, add the yoghurt, cumin, salt and milk.

2. Mix till smooth (the consistency should be like double cream). If you like it a little thinner just add a splash of milk and stir.

3. Add the diced onions, store in an airtight container and eat as required.

Lemon and Coriander Salad

This may sound strange but I always have a salad with a curry. And I know that you think that it's salad... what's the point? But I think you need to balance the flavours on your plate. Most Indian dishes are spicy, salty or sour, so a fresh salad helps to compliment those flavours. When I am visiting my sister she usually does the cooking and I end up being her sous chef. One of my jobs that I am still asked to do is to make the salad and I know if I dress it with fresh lemon and fresh coriander it gets eaten — after all that's the best compliment a cook can have.

PREPARATION TIME: 10 MINUTES   COOKING TIME: —   SERVES APPROX 6—8

Ingredients

¼ of an iceberg lettuce

2 medium sized tomatoes

Half a red onion

¼ cucumber

¼ tsp of salt

1 tsp freshly squeezed lemon juice

1 tsp fresh coriander leaves — finely chopped

Method

1. Wash and thoroughly drain the lettuce, tear the leaves into pieces (this helps it to remain crispy). Slicing with a metal knife can make the lettuce limp after a while. Put the lettuce into a large bowl.

2. Half the tomatoes and slice into pieces, slice the cucumber and add to bowl.

3. Finely slice the onions into half moons, they look prettier this way.

4. Add the salt, lemon juice, fresh coriander and gently mix together. Leave at room temperature for 10 minutes before serving.

Tomato and Lettuce Salad

This very simple salad works really well with starters such as fish pakoras and aloo tikka together with a cumin yoghurt. As long as the tomatoes are sweet and the lettuce is nice and crunchy. For best results make sure the tomatoes are room temperature, they taste even sweeter. I usually keep a few tomatoes in my fruit bowl after all aren't tomatoes actually a fruit?

PREPARATION TIME: 5 MINUTES	COOKING TIME: —	SERVES APPROX 6

Ingredients

¼ of an iceberg lettuce

2 medium sized tomatoes
or 10 cherry tomatoes

¼ tsp of salt

1 tsp freshly squeezed lemon juice

Method

1. Wash and thoroughly drain the lettuce, tear the leaves into pieces or slice with a plastic knife. Place the lettuce into a large bowl.

2. Wash the tomatoes and slice into pieces, add to the lettuce. If you are using cherry tomatoes, cut them in half.

3. Add the salt and lemon juice, gently mix together and serve at room temperature.

Minty Onions

Most Indian restaurants will serve a version of minty onions with their popadoms. Some restaurants dress them with a sweet mint sauce and some with slightly salty garden mint. I prefer the salty minty version myself. Again this quick cheeky little onion salad is served in contrast to the spicy starters and work amazingly well. If I want to have a salad with my curry and chapattis and don't have any salad in the house, I will quickly make some minty onions to have with my meal.

PREPARATION TIME: 5 MINUTES   COOKING TIME: —   SERVES APPROX 6

Ingredients

2 medium sized onions

½ tsp of garden mint

¼ tsp of salt

Method

1. Finely slice or dice the onions, whatever you prefer. Separate them out using your fingers and place in a small bowl.

2. Add the salt, garden mint and thoroughly mix together. Serve at room temperature with your starters or main meal.

Drinks

This may be the smallest section in the book but I think it's a vital section. After all we all love a cuppa after a meal, well I know that I do. Tea is such a British beverage but it's also a very Asian thing. So with both my Asian heritage and British upbringing it was a given that I would be a tea drinker.

I am well aware that when cooking an Indian meal, Indian drinks are not at the top of most people's priority. However, I feel that the trend is slowly changing; drinks like Chai Latte can be seen in many high street coffee shops and Mango Lassi seems to be increasingly gracing our supermarket shelves. Apart from my obligatory Cafe Latte, which is essential when I am out shopping, I still think that anything home-made tastes better. So give these a try. I think you will be pleasantly surprised at how delicious they are.

There are many recipes for all sorts of Indian drinks but I have again kept it quite simple and included the easiest drinks for you to re-create at home. Some, like the plain salt lassi, are simple and cooling on a hot summers day with an aloo paratha but others are similar to desserts and are quite sweet scented and fragrant. From the cardamom infused chai to the refreshing rose water floats, what's not to love!

Photograph by Jack Sharp

Kashmiri Chai Latte

*T*his creamy sweet tea is perfect with paratha on a cold winters day. For the health conscious out there you can halve the amount of sugar or serve without it and use semi skimmed milk if you prefer. I have noticed that in the last few years chai is becoming quite popular, many coffee houses now serve it and I have seen chai tea bags in many supermarkets. So why not follow the trend and make it for yourself. I sometimes call it chai latte, as when I first started catering one of my clients asked what chai was and I described it as a latte made with tea instead of coffee with an an ethnic twist.

PREPARATION TIME:	COOKING TIME: 10 MINUTES	SERVES APPROX 6

Ingredients

4 English breakfast tea bags

5 cardamom pods

1 pint cold water

1 pint of whole milk

5 tbsp sugar (optional)

Method

1. In a large saucepan, add the tea bags, milk, water, sugar and cardamom (split the pods in half, allowing the flavour to infuse into the tea). Then, stir with a tablespoon and bring to the boil.

2. Now turn the heat to low and simmer for 10 minutes or until the volume of liquid has reduced by a third. Stir every now and again and keep an eye on the tea, in case the milk boils over.

3. Using a fine metal tea strainer, pour tea into a teapot. Serve in tea cups or chai glasses.

Parveen's Top Tip

For a stronger flavour you can use loose black tea, just remember to sieve carefully before serving. For additional flavours, you can use cinnamon or ready made tea masala.

Rose Water Float

This is a modern take on a traditional sweet drink called Faluda, which is made with rose water syrup, milk and a few other things. It is one of my husband's favourite drinks and he first introduced me to it in the summer of "87", just a few weeks before we got married. However, this recipe is what my friend calls a "happy accident". I discovered this whilst I was catering a summer ball — as I accidently dropped the kulfi into the rose water milkshake. I have to say that it's one of the most popular desserts that I make for my dinner parties.

PREPARATION TIME: 5 MINUTES   COOKING TIME: —   SERVES APPROX 4—6

Ingredients

1 pint of whole milk

4 tbsp of pink rose water syrup

4 tsp of crushed pistachio

1 litre of pistachio kulfi

Silver edible glitter (optional)

Method

1. Pour the milk into a large jug and add the rose water, the milk will turn a lovely bright pink.

2. Pour the milkshake into either sundae glasses or I quite like martini glasses.

3. Scoop a heaped tablespoon of kulfi and place in the glass and you will find that it will float, hence the title.

4. To garnish: add crushed pistachio and some edible glitter for that glam factor. Serve immediately.

Parveen's Top Tip

Once the kulfi (Indian ice-cream) is added to the milk, it will melt quite quickly and adds more sweetness to the flavour. I usually serve in a glass with a small teaspoon, so my guests can scoop out the ice cream.

Salty Lassi

This is a perfect accompaniment for any spicy dish, providing a perfect palate cleanser. Salt lassi is traditionally served as a cool drink to hydrate and put salt back into the body. Whilst Indian summers are not commonplace here in the U.K., salt lassi hits the spot with a hot curry.

PREPARATION TIME: 2 TO 3 MINUTES	COOKING TIME: —	SERVES APPROX 4—6

Ingredients

500 g natural yoghurt

200 ml whole milk

200 ml water

½ tsp salt

Method

1. Add all the ingredients into a blender and blitz for 1 minute. Taste and adjust accordingly.

2. Chill and serve in a glass.

Sweet Lassi

To make Sweet Lassi, just substitute the salt for 2 tablespoons of sugar and hey presto, you have Sweet Lassi. There is no right or wrong when choosing a salt or sweet Lassi, its purely, personal preference.

Mango Lassi

*T*his sweet mango drink is popular in the summer months with all my children. For all intents and purposes — it's like a mango smoothie except it's traditionally made with yoghurt. It's quite a simple recipe and best of all it requires no cooking. Mango lassi is now readily available in many major supermarkets, however they do contain quite a lot of sugar and sometimes preservatives. I prefer to make it at home, it tastes so fresh and it will last in the fridge for a couple of days.

PREPARATION TIME: 5 MINUTES COOKING TIME: — SERVES APPROX 6

Ingredients

2 fresh mangoes (diced into 1 cm pieces)

100 ml single cream

200 ml whole milk

400 ml natural unsweetened yoghurt

4 tsp caster sugar

Method

1. To dice the mango; carefully cut down either side of the fattest part, sometimes called the "cheek." Take that piece and score lengthways and widthways, making small squares. Turn the skin inside out and you should have a mango that looks like a hedgehog. Cut out the juicy little cubes of mango.

2. Add the mango pieces into a blender together with the cream, milk, yoghurt and sugar, blitz together till smooth.

3. Have a taste and add a little more sugar if you like it sweeter or milk if you prefer a thinner consistency.

4. Chill, pour into tall glasses and serve.

Parveen's Top Tip

Although fresh mangoes are best, you can use tinned, frozen or mango pulp. For a richer flavour, you can add ice cream and if you are watching the calories, you can always leave out the cream and use semi-skimmed milk.

Desserts

I have such a sweet tooth… I just love desserts! So much so that when I go out to eat, the first thing I do is check out the dessert menu before I even decide what I am going to have for the mains. But the same does not seem to apply when "going out for an Indian". Many of my friends will not even bother ordering an Indian dessert or they will just have the obligatory kulfi (Indian ice-cream). I catered a charity event a few years ago and made a trio of desserts, one of my friends commented that she didn't realise that there was even one decent Indian dessert, let alone three! Well, I opened her eyes and her taste buds to something new and I would like to do the same for you. I want to broaden your horizons into the world of Asian sweet treats.

So, let's give home-made Indian desserts a chance… yes, they are extremely sweet, similar to Middle Eastern desserts. However, subtlety is not the name of the game when it comes to my culture or my cuisine. In my humble opinion, we are quite dramatic, we wear colourful, vibrant clothes, use dramatic hand gestures (well, I know I do) and yes our spicy food is spicy and sweets are sweet. Therefore I felt it quite necessary to include a traditional dessert section in the book. Many of the desserts are very fragrant and contain ingredients like cardamom, coconut and rose water, which not only taste good, but have a lovely aroma — how wonderful is that.

Kheer (Cardamom Rice Pudding)

This creamy, fragrant version of an Asian rice pudding can be served at any occasion for dessert all year round. I serve it warm on cold days and chilled on summer days, so it's a win-win really. Kheer is a popular dish at weddings when there are 500 plus mouths to feed; it goes down a treat. There are various recipes for this dish, however, in my opinion I think this is the easiest. As with many of my desserts I like to add a touch of glamour by dusting it with some edible glitter.

PREPARATION TIME: 5 MINUTES	COOKING TIME: 40 MINUTES	SERVES APPROX 6

Ingredients

1 litre whole milk

2 heaped tbsp of pudding or risotto rice

4 cardamom pods — opened

3 tbsp of caster sugar

2 tbsp of crushed pistachios — to decorate

2 tbsp of flaked almonds

Method

1. Pour the milk into a heavy based pan, add the rice, sugar and cardamom pods, turn heat on high and bring to the boil.

2. When the milk is boiling, turn heat down to low and simmer for about 1 hour, stirring every 5 to 10 minutes to prevent the rice and milk sticking to the bottom of the pan.

3. You will notice that the buttermilk rises to the top and creates a skin, you can remove this, or just leave it if your prefer.

4. After an hour, the milk will have reduced down by half. You will now have a single cream consistency and the rice will have fluffed up and absorbed all the sweet milk.

5. Take out the cardamom pods and add half the flaked almonds. If you prefer it a little sweeter; just add another tablespoon of sugar and simmer for a further 5 minutes.

6. Decanter into a serving bowl and serve at the desired temperature, sprinkled with crushed pistachio and flaked almonds and of course if you have it.. a little glitter.

Parveen's Top Tip

To give the kheer extra texture, add 2 tbsp of desiccated coconut half way through the simmering process. Sultanas can also be added for texture and flavour, again just add a couple of tablespoons half way through the simmering process.

Dry Sweet Vermicelli (Sevia)

This is one of my husband's favourite Asian desserts. This dish is usually served on special occasions like "Eid" (Muslim festival, similar to Christmas) and often a popular dessert when I have guests for dinner. It's one of the easier Asian desserts and not too heavy going. I usually serve my sevia in small glass dessert bowls, alongside chai lattes or just English breakfast tea... well, I do love a cup of tea!

PREPARATION TIME:	COOKING TIME: 30MINS	SERVES APPROX 6

Ingredients

150 g medium vermicelli

100 g caster sugar

4 cardamom pods — opened

50 g butter

100 ml boiling water

Method

1. In a medium sized pan, gently melt butter on very low heat, ensuring it does not burn (if the butter burns, it will add a bitter aftertaste to the cooked sevia).

2. Gently crush the vermicelli in your hands and add to the butter. On a medium heat, using a clean wooden spoon, thoroughly stir the vermicelli making sure all the pieces are covered in the butter.

3. Turn the heat on high and keep stirring the vermicelli until nearly all strands are a golden brown, this will take about 5 minutes.

4. Add boiling water, sugar and cardamom pods, stir a few times and bring everything to the boil. Turn the heat down to low, cover with a lid and simmer for 30 minutes.

5. Now take the lid off and you will notice that the vermicelli has absorbed all the water. Gently loosen pieces with a fork and serve hot, with tea.

Parveen's Top Tip

Again as with the milky vermicelli, you can use fine vermicelli, just cut down the simmering time (stage 4) to 10 minutes. A good way of testing to see if it is cooked is to take out a piece of vermicelli and squash it between your finger and thumb, it should easily break, if it is still a little al dente, just put the lid on and simmer for a further 5 to 10 minutes, test using the same method.

Milky Sweet Vermicelli

*T*his fragrant sweet dessert is usually served on special occasions and was a must at our house for breakfast on Eid (festival similar to Christmas). I can remember, as a child waking up on Eid mornings to the smell of gently simmering cardamom milk wafting through the house. Even now I associate that sweet smell with happy times on Eid with my brothers and sisters. Following the family tradition, 3 decades on, guess what? That's right I make milky sevia for my children on Eid morning.

PREPARATION TIME:	COOKING TIME: 35 MINUTES	SERVES APPROX 6

Ingredients

150 g medium vermicelli

1 pint of whole milk

100 g caster sugar

4 cardamom pods — opened

30 g butter

Method

1. Use a medium sized pasta pan, add the butter and gently melt on a low heat, ensuring it does not burn.

2. Crush the vermicelli gently in your hands and add to the butter on a medium heat, gently stir the vermicelli for 5 minutes. Some of the strands of vermicelli will turn light golden brown (use a wooden spoon as this makes it easier to stir).

3. Slowly pour the milk over the vermicelli, be very careful of hot splatters as the milk reacts with the hot pan. Then add the sugar and cardamom pods. Turn heat onto high and bring to the boil.

4. Once boiling, turn onto lowest heat and simmer for about 30 minutes. Stir occasionally, you will notice that the buttermilk rises to the top and creates a skin, you can remove this, or just leave it if you prefer.

5. The milk will have reduced down and will now have a single cream consistency and the vermicelli will be cooked. You can serve it hot or cold, sprinkled with crushed pistachio nuts.

Parveen's Top Tip

If you want to serve this dish cold or at room temperature first decanter it into a bowl and cover tightly with cling film thus ensuring that the sevia does not form skin on the surface. For this recipe you can use fine vermicelli, just cut down stage 2 to 3 minutes and simmering time to 20 minutes.

Halva

Many Asian and Middle Eastern cuisines have their own versions of Halva. I was lucky enough to travel to Greece to cook with some chefs and was astounded when I learnt that the recipe called for 400% sugar. I do like to eat halva but I am always mindful of the amount of sugar, so my recipe is just sweet enough to give you a sugar rush!

PREPARATION TIME:	COOKING TIME: 50 MINUTES	SERVES APPROX 6

Ingredients

250 g course or fine semolina

200 g sugar

150 g butter

5 green cardamom or ½ tsp of cardamom powder

1 tbsp flaked almonds

2 tbsp raisins or sultanas

750 ml hot water

Method

1. In a medium sized pan, add the hot water and dissolve the sugar. Add the cardamom pods, just open them slightly first.

2. Simmer the sugar mixture for 20 minutes.

3. While the water is simmering, take another heavy based saucepan and melt the butter on the lowest heat, taking care not to burn it as it can burn quite easily and this will give you a bitter taste. Now add the semolina, on medium heat using a wooden spoon, stir-fry the semolina for 10 minutes or until it turns a light golden brown. Keep stirring do not let the semolina settle at the bottom of the pan as it can burn quite easily.

4. Turn the heat to low and slowly pour the sugary water into the semolina, stirring as you pour. Be very careful of hot splatters as the water reacts to the semolina. The semolina will absorb all the water and will have the consistency of thin porridge.

5. Turn the heat onto high and stir continuously for about 10 minutes. The liquid will reduce and the semolina will become thicker and take on a glossy appearance as the butter rises to the top.

6. Add half the almonds and sultanas and cook for a further 5 minutes on a low heat, stirring every now and again. Cover with lid and simmer on the lowest of heat for the last 5 minutes. Serve warm, garnished with the almonds and sultanas.

Parveen's Top Tip

For the sake of ease, use a pan with a long handle, as this will keep your hands away from any hot splatters.

Ghajar Ka Halva

This rich dessert is usually made on special festivals such as Eid. It's made from fresh carrots, so I could describe it as an Asian version of carrot cake. There are many different recipes but this is the simplest to follow. My sister taught me how to make this recipe and I have to say her Ghajar Ka Halva is just the best, it's delicious. She is extremely famous for it, in fact friends and family will pop round for a visit just to enjoy her Ghajar Ka Halva. I think she uses our mother's favourite ingredient — Love.

PREPARATION TIME: 10 MINUTES | COOKING TIME: 40 MINUTES | SERVES APPROX 6

Ingredients

8 medium sized carrots — finely grated

1 litre of whole milk

60 g butter

150 ml double cream

12 tbsp sugar

2 tbsp chopped almonds

2 tbsp crushed pistachio nuts

6 green cardamom pods or ½ tsp of powdered cardamom

2 tbsp golden raisins

Method

1. In a deep, heavy based pan add the carrots and bring to the boil, then steam through for 4 to 5 minutes allowing their natural water to cook out. Then add the sugar, milk and cardamom pods (slightly open the pods first).

2. Bring the carrot mixture to a boil then simmer on a low heat for 15 to 20 minutes or until the milk has almost evaporated.

3. While the carrots are simmering, keep an eye on the milk in case it boils over, stirring every 4 to 5 minutes.

4. Now add the butter, cream and stir. Turn heat to high and stir fry the carrot mixture allowing it to cook in the butter for 10 to 15 minutes, stirring occasionally. Make sure it doesn't stick to the bottom of the pan, if it does, just turn the heat down a little.

5. The liquid will now have evaporated and the carrots will have broken down and the mixture will be a deep golden orange colour. Add the almonds, pistachio nuts and raisins, then simmer on low for a further 10 minutes, allowing the butter to rise to the surface.

6. Serve warm with cream or ice-cream.

Parveen's Top Tip

It's always best to use fresh carrots, however frozen can be an alternative. Although I personally think that frozen carrots retain their water which affects the taste of the dish.

Sweet Rice

This golden, orange-coloured, sweet rice is served on special occasions and is very popular at Asian weddings — probably because it can be easily cooked en masse. Many people add lots of dried fruit, cherries, raisins and sultanas. I prefer to add a small amount of flaked almonds and pistachios, mostly because my husband likes to taste the rice rather than the dried fruit.

PREPARATION TIME: —   COOKING TIME: 40 MINUTES   SERVES APPROX 8

Ingredients

- 500 g of white basmati rice
- 150 g butter
- 200 g sugar
- 2 tbsp of finely sliced pistachio nuts
- 2 tbsp of flaked almonds
- 1 tsp yellow food colouring
- 6 cardamom pods — opened

Method

1. Place the rice in a large bowl. Gently wash the rice through 4 times or until the water runs clear. Soak the rice for 2 hours in cool water.

2. In a large pan with a lid, add 1 litre of boiling water. Then add the food colouring, drained rice, and the cardamom pods, simmer for 20 minutes or until rice is al dente.

3. Drain the rice, which will be a bright orangey colour and set aside in an open bowl.

4. Using the same pan, add butter, sugar and 4 tbsp of water, gently melt together. Once boiled, turn down to a simmer and cook through for 5 to 7 minutes. The water will reduce and you will now have a buttery coloured caramel.

5. Add the boiled rice back into the pan. Add half of the pistachio and almonds, gently stir 3 times with a wooden spoon, covering all the rice with the lovely sweet caramel.

6. Cover with the lid and simmer for 10 minutes, allowing all the flavours to infuse. Serve warm or hot, topped with the rest of the pistachios and almonds.

Parveen's Top Tip

To keep the nuts nice and crispy you can add them at step 6 and just give them 10 minutes to cook through.

Mango Mess

*T*his recipe was discovered by my very good friend Jeannie. I was catering for a Bollywood Summer Garden Party and Jeannie was helping me plan the desserts as she is an excellent baker. The client did not want a typical Asian desert but wanted something sweet, tasty, summery and ethnic. After a few ideas, Jeannie came up with mango mess, which my clients loved, I then made it for her 50 guests. It went down a treat. I served it in crystal martini glasses topped with white glitter; well I am all about the bling!

PREPARATION TIME: 10 MINUTES	COOKING TIME: 10 MINUTES	SERVES APPROX 10

Ingredients

500 ml whipping cream

200 g tinned mango pulp

2 medium sized mangoes

8 ready-made meringue nests (5 x 7 cm)

2 tbsp of caster sugar

Method

1. Peel the mangoes and dice into 1 cm cubes, see photo for tips on how to peel mangoes.

2. In a large bowl, add the sugar to the cream and whip till stiff peaks are formed, you can do this by hand or using an electric mixer, I do it by hand, doesn't take very long to be honest.

3. Carefully crush the meringues into the cream, add the mango pieces and fold mixture together.

4. Into small dessert bowls, or I like to use martini glasses, add approximately 2 heaped tbsp of the mixture and drizzle mango pulp on top as a dressing.

5. Sprinkle with a little edible silver glitter and serve immediately.

Parveen's Top Tip

If you cannot get hold of any fresh mangoes, you can use either tinned or frozen, but these days, I have noticed that the major supermarkets sell fresh fruit already peeled and cut in the fresh fruit section and these are available throughout the year. I personally prefer Pakistani mangoes, they are as sweet as nectar and not at all "stringy" but the problem is that they are only in season from about May to July.

Fruit Chaat

This is fundamentally a fruit salad with a bite. The salt, pepper and lemon juice helps to bring out the flavours in the fruit. Try and use fresh, seasonal fruits as they taste so much better. But as a last resort, tinned fruit works quite well. Actually for my recipe, I prefer to use tinned guavas as the juice creates a deliciously rich, sweet sauce for the fruit to swim in.

PREPARATION TIME: 15 TO 20 MINUTES	COOKING TIME: —	SERVES APPROX 6

Ingredients

1 large mango

1 pomegranate

2 apples (any variety)

2 small bananas

1 small bunch of seedless green grapes

200 g of tinned guava

1 large orange

1 tsp fresh lemon juice

¼ tsp salt

¼ tsp fine black pepper

Method

1. Firstly, you need to peel and chop the fruit, ready to assemble in a large bowl.

2. Take seeds out of the pomegranate, the easiest way is to slice off the top and bottom and cut in half. Hold each half over a bowl, and very firmly tap the back with a serving spoon, the jewels of pomegranate will just pop out.

3. Peel and core the apples into 1 cm cubes; wash and half the grapes; cut the orange into half; peel and dice half into 1 cm cubes and juice the rest. Lastly peel the bananas and cut into 1 cm slices.

4. Add all the fruit to the bowl. Slice the guavas in half, add to mix and use the juice to create a delicious fruity sauce.

5. Lastly, add the juice of the lemon, salt and pepper. Gently mix together and serve chilled or even better at room temperature.

Parveen's Top Tip

Almost any fruits can be used but only certain ones really work together. And of course I use a range of exotic fruits but you can easily make this with just apples, pears, bananas and grapes for a basic fruit chaat.

How to order at an Indian Restaurant

I was asked to write this section of the book by Jeannie, a very dear friend of mine who is a wonderful home cook and fabulous baker, in fact her cakes are the best I have ever had! She has a good knowledge of ingredients from other cultures and owns over 200 cook books, but take her out of the safe haven of her own kitchen and land her on a ruby red chair in the middle of our local Indian restaurant and she is clueless! Every time we eat out, she looks at me with a helpless, "what shall we order" kind of look.

Firstly, I just want to say that food served in the restaurant trade is very different to home cooked Indian food like the recipes in this cook book. Restaurants have to serve large quantities very quickly and sometimes the quality is compromised. They often use the same curry sauce base for several dishes which is why at times the dishes taste a bit "samey." You will probably not have authentic dishes unless you want to pay to eat in a Michelin Star Indian restaurant where all the dishes are freshly prepared and cooked to order. Most of my non-Asian girlfriends say that they are not 100% sure of what goes with what and because they are unsure they end up ordering their usual dishes and don't tend to experiment or deviate. So this quick guide to ordering in a restaurant is for those of you who want try something different.

Plus a few do's and don'ts in my humble opinion.

My first major tip has to be try and find an Indian restaurant that is frequented by Asians, then you know it will be authentic!

Chef's Recommendation

Get to know your waiter, ask for their name and what dishes they would suggest. Ask questions such as which dishes are freshly cooked that day or what the chef recommends. Remember, the waiter may not have tasted all of the dishes but the chefs will have; they cooked them after all. Often, main dishes such as the curries will be cooked a day in advance and stored in the fridge. But that's ok, we all know that curry tastes even better the day after it's cooked!

Ordering Vegetable Dishes

With vegetable dishes, again ask the waiter which vegetables are fresh that day. Many restaurants will use frozen and sometimes tinned. However, some tinned vegetables are still tasty when cooked. A chickpea masala for example is as flavoursome as the real thing, if not better! Also, some vegetables are quite acceptable frozen, i.e. peas and sweet corn, but others like cauliflower (gobi), aubergine and courgettes really need to be fresh.

Share Food

Do mix and match, this is very appropriate for Indian cuisine, which is designed to be shared. I know many people who do this and I think it really adds to the variety. But if some members of your party like it hot and you want to share the same dish; order a mild curry and then ask the waiter for a hot sauce, this is usually in the form of a green chilli dip. Use the dip as an accompaniment, just add a teaspoon on the side of your own plate and that will give you the heat you need.

Popadoms

I love popadoms but as an Asian housewife and private chef, I have never actually served them at my dinner parties. I make them as snacks at times. However, in Indian restaurants they are designed to be served to help pass the time whilst your order is being made. The condiments accompanying popadoms are delicious but can be quite salty, which makes you drink too much. Instead, just have a little and try and save yourself for the main meal.

That Bloated Feeling

Don't fill up on naan bread! Naan is made with white flour and yeast; which tends to be quite filling and you may leave the restaurant feeling a little bloated. I know where you are coming from though — as a hot buttered naan bread is addictive! A good alternative are chapattis, they contain no salt, yeast or butter.

Some Like it HOT or NOT

If you don't like your food too spicy, then order plain boiled rice, which helps to soak up the spicy curry sauce, stay away from Biryani which is made with chillies. And if it is really too hot and your mouth is on fire, don't be tempted to drink water as all this does is disperse the chilli around the mouth and makes matters worse. Instead have a few tablespoons of the cucumber raita or a minty yoghurt sauce. These condiments are specifically designed to cool down the mouth; yoghurt is cooling, cucumber is cooling and mint is cooling, so it's a triple whammy on the senses!

Portion Control

Whilst eating out I often see people eating a curry just by itself, using a fork and eating it like a stew. Traditionally curry is meant to be about a quarter of the meal in terms of proportionality. Try balancing out your meal equally with rice/naan/chapattis, salad and yoghurt. Your senses will not be overwhelmed by spice this way.

Salad — Really!

I think the most misunderstood category of food in Indian restaurants is salad. I know many of my friends will not bother with it. But salad is served with the dishes for a good reason. Again, it's to cool down the palate and the freshness is in complete contrast to the deep rich spicy flavours of the curry. At home or at my dinner parties, I would not dream of serving a meal without a crispy fresh salad. Next time you are in an Indian restaurant, try the salad with the spicy food, it really compliments it.

Variety is the Spice of Life

When ordering your dishes I know the menu can be overwhelming but if you read the ingredients of the dishes carefully, you will notice many will be similar. So order a variety; try and include white meat, red meat, vegetables and pulses along with the usual suspects of naan and rice. For example, if you order a chicken dish for the starter have a lamb dish for mains or vice versa, then add one vegetable or lentil curry.

Vegetarians and Vegans

Indian cuisine lends itself so well to vegetarianism and veganism. The only difference for vegans would be that they cannot eat the yoghurt dips or the paneer. Otherwise there is a wide range of vegetable curries to choose from, the old favourites like aloo gobi, saag aloo, okra, daal, chickpeas etc, as well as vegetarian starters, like onion bhajis, vegetable samosas, spicy potato cakes etc.

Gluten-Free Ordering

Having a wheat allergy can be a problem. However with Indian food you have quite a wide range of dishes to choose from. All the rice dishes and all the curries will be gluten free, as flour is not usually used as a thickener. But take care when ordering the starters, any bhaji or pakora will be safe as they are made with chickpea flour. Also a quick bit of trivia about bhajis and pakoras, they are the same thing, just different dialects. Bhaji is a Hindi word and Pakora is the Punjabi name for a Bhaji. Take care with samosas as the pastry will be made with wheat flour. However, be careful of having a tandoori chicken starter as flour may be used to coat the chicken. If unsure, just ask your waiter.

Dishes That Work Well Together

Use the menu planner of p. 157 to help you order dishes that work well together. Whether you are cooking recipes from this cook book or eating out, the same principle applies.

Menu Planner

E ven as an experienced cook, the hardest part of my job is deciding what to cook. It's not always easy to know what dishes to serve with what. To make life a little easier, and I am all for that, here are some menus I put together for you. I have not included desserts as I think any sweet dish is lovely after a meal.

Menu 1
(Popular Dishes)

....

Starters
Onion Bhajis
with
Minty Yoghurt
And
Tomato & Onion Salad

....

Mains
Chicken Masala
Tarka Daal

Naan

Pilau Rice With Peas & Potatoes

Cucumber Raita

Menu 2
(Vegetarian)

....

Starters
Chick Pea Chaat
with
Cumin Yoghurt
And
Tamarind Sauce

....

Mains
Mixed Vegetable Curry
Saag Aloo

Chapattis

Cumin Buttered Rice

Minty Yoghurt

Menu 3
(Meat Lovers)

....

Starters
Lamb Sheesh Kebabs
with
Cumin Roast Potatoes
Green Chilli Dip
Minty Onions

....

Mains
Keema Aloo Mattar
Lamb Bhuna

Peshwari Naan

Chicken Pilau

Cucumber Raita

INDEX

Your Notes